Creating a
Marriage
You'll Love

Dedication

For Gertrude, Iola, Lilyan, and Ida,
the guiding lights who'll always be with me.

Sellers Publishing, Inc.
161 John Roberts Road, South Portland, Maine 04106
For ordering information:
(800) 625-3386 toll-free
(207) 772-6814 fax

Visit our Web site: www.sellerspublishing.com • E-mail: rsp@rsvp.com

Cover design by Rita Sowins

Interior design by Faceout Studio

ISBN 13: 978-1-4162-0559-3
Library of Congress Control Number: 2009931918

10 9 8 7 6 5 4 3 2 1

Printed in the United States of America.

Credits: Page 238

SECRETS FOR BUILDING A RICH
AND FULL LIFE TOGETHER

Creating a
Marriage
You'll Love

EDITED BY MARK CHIMSKY-LUSTIG

SELLERS
PUBLISHING

Contents

INTRODUCTION ✒ *page 8*

Harriet Lerner, Ph.D.
HOW TO CREATE A REMARKABLE MARRIAGE ✒ *page 17*

Judith S. Wallerstein, Ph.D. & Sandra Blakeslee
HAPPY MARRIAGES: DO THEY EXIST? ✒ *page 31*

John Gray, Ph.D.
DANCE STEPS FOR LASTING INTIMACY ✒ *page 47*

Terri Orbuch, Ph.D.
HOW TO HAVE A LOVING MARRIAGE, EVEN WITH LESS MONEY,
LESS TIME, AND MORE STRESS ✒ *page 59*

Gay Hendricks, Ph.D.
HOW TO CREATE A CONSCIOUS, LOVING MARRIAGE:
THE SEVEN KEYS ✒ *page 73*

Seth Meyers, Psy.D.
CREATING LOVE THAT LASTS ✒ *page 79*

Kristine Carlson
THE SMALL THINGS WE DID THAT NOURISHED
A LIFETIME OF LOVE ✒ *page 91*

Nicole Chaison
THE MARRIAGE TRIP *page 101*

Joseph Bailey
TRUE LOVE *page 115*

Nava Atlas
SECRET RECIPES FOR A SUCCESSFUL MARRIAGE *page 137*

John Van Epp, Ph.D.
THE HEALTHY IMBALANCED MARRIAGE *page 143*

Lindsey Rietzsch
LOVE AS A LIFESTYLE *page 157*

Scott Haltzman, M.D.
COOKING UP A RICH AND FULFILLING MARRIAGE *page 169*

Joel Crohn, Ph.D.
MIXED MATCHES: CREATING SUCCESSFUL INTERRACIAL,
INTERETHNIC, AND INTERFAITH RELATIONSHIPS *page 177*

Amanda Kane, L.S.W.
FIVE TACTICS FOR CREATING YOUR
BEST MARRIAGE *page 187*

Mike Robbins
BE THEIR BIGGEST FAN AND GREATEST CRITIC ✺ *page 199*

Barbara De Angelis, Ph.D.
MAKING THE CHOICE TO LOVE NOW ✺ *page 215*

Debra Galant
THE NUPTIAL CAR ✺ *page 229*

ABOUT THE AUTHOR ✺ *page 236*

ACKNOWLEDGMENTS ✺ *page 237*

CREDITS ✺ *page 238*

INTRODUCTION

What makes a marriage work? With apologies to Tolstoy, I believe every happy marriage is happy in its own way. My favorite response to this opening question comes from the late Kitty Carlisle Hart, wife of the famed Broadway director Moss Hart and known to 1960s TV viewers as the impeccably dressed, sophisticated panelist on the game show, *To Tell the Truth*. When asked what made her marriage to Hart so successful, Kitty immediately responded, "Good table manners." As if there couldn't *possibly* be any other explanation . . .

Marriage is a country that two people create and inhabit, a mysterious place with its own unique boundaries, rules, and language (both spoken and not). Some couples appear to be true soul mates, sharing passions and idiosyncrasies, while others seem to thrive on the differences between them, as if engaging in a high-stakes competitive sport.

Whatever we understand about marriage in the abstract, we usually know less than we think we do about the specifics of other people's marriages. We can make presumptions, but the fact is that each marriage is subject to its own peculiar laws. The public face may not match the private one at all. A happy marriage for one couple may, in truth, thrive on terms and conditions that would wreak havoc with another couple. So what is the constant that is common to all good marriages? Can there even *be* a constant that unites them? Studies have been done that suggest that respect, humor, empathy, and the ability to compromise may be the necessary essentials that any couple needs for a marriage to succeed. But what is the right balance of ingredients to make a marriage work — not only at first but over time?

The nature of marriage has evolved over centuries. We would be mistaken to view ancient marriages through a modern lens that emphasizes romance above all else. Early marriages were about economics, heirs, and property rights. While there were certainly love matches throughout history, before the mid-1800s it was common for couples to enter into matrimony without necessarily feeling it was a marriage of true hearts. As historian Stephanie Coontz notes, "For thousands of years marriage was a strong institution because no one expected it to be a very satisfying relationship." In many parts of the world it was (and still is) common for marriages to be arranged, with parents selecting a spouse for a daughter or son in order to increase landholdings, climb the social ladder, or use the alliance to gain more prominence in the community. According to Coontz, love was simply not considered a vital part of the equation.

In Shakespeare's time, it must have been fairly radical for the fourteen-year-old Juliet to reject the arranged match her parents had made for her with the princely Paris in favor of a marriage based on white-hot romance with that young Romeo fellow from a rival family. Jump ahead a few centuries from Verona, Italy, to the little *shtetl* of Anatevka in Eastern Europe. See how

Fiddler on the Roof's Tevye the milkman treads lightly as he asks his wife, Golde, if she loves him: it isn't a question that's come up in all their twenty-five years together. "Love," Tevye remarks, with a hint of astonishment. "A new word."

Now that marriage is less about collective bargaining and more about individual hearts courting and sparking, how is the flame kept burning bright? If our expectations about marriage are higher because we've invested so much in the idea of romance lasting over time, how do we keep the institution strong when love, by its very nature, is changeable?

The question, *How do two people sustain a marriage successfully?* became a kind of personal mantra as I developed *Creating a Marriage You'll Love.* With enough couples taking the plunge over the centuries, you'd think we'd have a pretty solid road map by now of how to make a marriage work. And yet, it still seems to be a mystery; answers are elusive. There's not just one yellow brick road that's certain to lead to the Oz of wedded bliss.

Because there seemed to be so many possible answers to my question I decided to seek essays from a diverse range of contributors — esteemed experts who've counseled countless couples; bestselling authors who've illuminated the dark corners of marriage; social psychologists, motivational speakers, and life coaches who've reflected on the nature of relationships and come up with their own ideas about the sustainability of love, our greatest and most unpredictable natural resource. I also sought out authors who had *not* made a profession of working with couples, but who could write personally about the *experience* of marriage, evoking the rich, fraught, hopeful reality of it.

Contributors seemed genuinely excited about the idea of looking afresh at the question of what makes a marriage fulfilling — and enduring. The roster of writers who agreed to contribute material ultimately included highly regarded professionals in the field and bestselling authors as well as an innovative graphic novelist, an acclaimed fiction writer, and a popular cookbook author. Of the total number of essays in the book, more than three-quarters are newly commissioned, appearing in print for the first time.

When the completed essays began showing up in my email inbox — a few even ahead of schedule! — I was immediately struck by the way some of the experts looked at their own marriages with candor as they wrote about the universals of married life. For example, in Harriet Lerner's "How to Create a Remarkable Marriage," she shows how she and her husband set the ground rules for communicating with respect, establishing "a bottom-line position about what we can or can't live with." John Van Epp's "The Healthy Imbalanced Marriage" describes the hazards of living with two partners — "the partner in your home and the partner in your head" — the real spouse and the warts-only version. He illustrates the panic that ensues when he allows his own escalating fears to get the better of him.

Sometimes, writing from a personal perspective can create a sense of the wonderful gifts marriage can bring to both partners. In her moving essay, "The Small Things We Did That Nourished a Lifetime of Love," Kristine Carlson takes the reader inside her happy marriage to see how — and why — it flourished before it was cut short by the untimely death of her husband, bestselling author Richard Carlson.

Other authors mine the humor to be found in marriage's ups and downs. Nicole Chaison's graphic essay, "The Marriage Trip," provides a delightfully loopy look at one woman's quest to figure out the secret to keeping a marriage passionate when it starts to plateau. Debra Galant's essay, "The Nuptial Car," resonates with wry home truths about married life and reveals how the promise of the first, post-wedding car ride can help us weather a road that may get bumpy later on.

〄 〄 〄

One of the ways we learn to sustain a marriage is by seeing how others do it. If one's own family of origin doesn't always provide the answer, sometimes the marriages of relatives or friends and neighbors do. For some of us of a particular age, we turned to our TV sets. Back before the advent of lurid reality shows featuring desperate housewives, TV was the medium that revealed the secrets of how other families lived.

As a kid growing up in Cincinnati, Ohio, I loved the accessible urbanity of *The Dick Van Dyke Show's* Rob and Laura Petrie, a couple played by Dick Van Dyke and Mary Tyler Moore with enough chemistry to heat up the Philco. They had a youthful spontaneity and seemed to delight in the thrill of being in love in a way that was different from the old-shoe comfiness of real-life married couples like Ozzie and Harriet and Roy Rogers and Dale Evans. Though Rob and Laura slept in separate beds, you had the feeling that was just to keep the censors happy — you didn't believe they *really* wanted a two-bed marriage.

I was intrigued by the way television provided a portal into the lives of all kinds of married couples. Sure, I could observe my parents and their friends, but it was much more fun to see how TV couples sparred and parried: I could follow Ward and June Cleaver of *Leave It to Beaver* or Jim and Margaret Anderson of *Father Knows Best* into their bedrooms to hear what married people actually said to each other when they bickered about the kids or revealed secrets or resolved their issues with a kiss. Some couples seemed too good to be true (as a teenager I had a certain skepticism about Mr. and Mrs. Brady Bunch, who seemed like Barbie and Ken dolls sprung to life). Still, I found that even the most broadly comic, idealized couples had some lessons to teach — if I looked hard enough.

I learned a lot from TV couples — after all, watch enough sitcoms and you gain a kind of master's in marriage —

    ✥ from **Lucy and Ricky Ricardo** of *I Love Lucy*, I learned that a bit of zany unpredictability can keep a marriage from going stale. A dose of Vitameatavegamin, anyone?

✺ from **Samantha and Darren Stephens** of *Betwitched*, I learned that even in the wilds of Westport, Connecticut, you can have a fulfilling fantasy life that has nothing to do with your partner.

✺ from *All in the Family's* **Edith and Archie Bunker**, I learned about the way couples balance each other — and soften one another's rough edges. Would we really like the bigoted Archie quite so much if he wasn't paired with Edith, his conscience-in-residence?

✺ from *The Cosby Show's* **Cliff and Claire Huxtable**, I learned that intelligence and an unflappable sense of humor can help you deal with anything, even five rambunctious kids.

✺ from **Roseanne and Dan Conner** of *Roseanne*, I learned that it's okay to be raucously in love and frighteningly honest about how you feel — and to not always have all the answers.

✺ from **Homer and Marge Simpson** of *The Simpsons*, I learned that love is blind and sometimes there's just no rhyme or reason as to what makes a marriage tick.

One of the happiest marriages to make its way onto the big screen is portrayed in Nora Ephron's recent frothy movie *Julie & Julia* about two couples, two time periods, and plowing one's way through the 524 recipes in *Mastering the Art of French Cooking, Vol. 1*, by Julia Child, Simone Beck, and Louisette Bertholle, in 365 days. One of the real-life marriages depicted is that of Julia and Paul Child (played in the film by Meryl Streep and Stanley Tucci), who had a zest for both eating and loving. One scene in particular stands out: Julia and Paul are frolicking in a bubble bath posing for their annual holiday card. They gesture towards one another adoringly — the no-nonsense Julia and the staid diplomat Paul are joyously playful. It's not just the bubble bath but their love that seems to make them uncharacteristically giddy.

As this moment is captured on their card, we see the greeting that is imprinted on it — "Wish you were here." At first, the phrase registers just as a bit of spicy double entendre, but long after the scene was over I found myself thinking about that line and how the film's Julia and Paul might be wishing that their friends (and by extension, us) could be in the "here" of a happy marriage, delighting in the tender, exuberant affection of a soul mate looking on lovingly nearby.

My wish for all of you reading *Creating a Marriage You'll Love* is that you'll find in these pages a taste of the "here" of happy marriages. The insights and wisdom of the contributors to this book will hopefully provide you with excellent food for thought. So mind your table manners and as Julia Child would say, "Bon appétit!"

Mark Chimsky-Lustig
January 2010

HARRIET LERNER, PH.D., is one of our nation's most trusted and respected experts on marriage and family relationships. She is the author of numerous scholarly articles and ten books, including the *New York Times* bestseller, *The Dance of Anger*, *The Dance of Intimacy*, and most recently, *The Dance of Fear*. Lerner travels nationally to lecture, consult, and present workshops, and she has has been a guest on *The Oprah Winfrey Show*, CNN, NPR, and numerous other media. She is a blogger for *Psychology Today*, and, in collaboration with her sister, she's an award-winning children's book author.

How to Create
a Remarkable Marriage
Harriet Lerner, Ph.D.

A story is told about two little kids who are playing together in a sand-box with their pails and shovels. Suddenly a huge fight breaks out and one of them runs away screaming, "I hate you! I hate you!" In no time at all they're back in the sandbox playing together happily again.

Two adults observe the interaction from a nearby bench. "Did you see that?" one comments in admiration. "How do children do that? They were enemies five minutes ago."

"It's simple," the other replies. "They chose happiness over righteousness."

Grownups rarely make such a choice. Married folks often have a terrible time stepping aside from anger, bitterness, and hurt. We know that life is short, but damn it, we're not getting back in that sandbox until the other person agrees to having started it and ad-mits to being wrong. Our need to balance the scales of justice is so strong that we may lock ourselves into negativity at the expense of happiness and well-being.

A great deal of suffering could be avoided if we could be more like those kids. I feel calmed and relieved when my husband knocks at my study door in the middle of a fight, put his arms around me, and says, "I love you. This is stupid. Let's just drop it." Like two kids in the sandbox, we're light and playful again.

Of course, married life is not always so simple as the sandbox story. To get to the place where we can lighten up and let things go, we need the capacity to speak with a strong voice and to listen with an open heart. When people have an "anything goes" policy in marriage, things can only spiral downhill.

The challenge then is to lighten up *and* to have a strong voice when the situation calls for it. Let's look at what each of these challenges requires of us.

Part I: MOVING TOWARD LIGHTNESS

The following seven steps will help you move toward more lightness (rather than more intensity) in your marriage. Remember, what's important is the direction you move in over time — not the speed of travel. Real change in marriage is usually a slow and bumpy process that takes patience and time. If you try to change too much too fast, you will stir up too much anxiety (your own included) and nothing will change at all.

Get More Bite Marks on Your Tongue

Speaking our minds and hearts is at the core of intimacy. We all long to have a marriage that is so relaxed and intimate that we can share anything and everything without thinking about it. Who wants to hide out in a relationship in which we can't allow ourselves to be known? I've yet to meet the person who aspires to be phony or silent in her marriage. The dictate to "Be Yourself" is a cultural ideal and, luckily, no one else is as qualified for the job.

But speaking out and being "real" are not always good ideas. Sometimes in the name of authenticity and truth-telling, we shut down the lines of communication, diminish and shame the other person, and make it less likely that we'll hear each other or even be able to stay in the same room. We may talk a particular subject to death, or focus on the negative in a way that draws us deeper into it when we'd be better off distracting ourselves and going to the movies.

Try to make wise and thoughtful decisions about how and when to say what to your partner. Timing and tact in marriage is not the opposite of honesty. Rather, it is what makes honesty possible.

Respect Differences

One of my favorite cartoons, drawn by my friend Jennifer Berman, shows a dog and a cat in bed together.

The dog is looking morose and reading a book called *Dogs Who Love Too Much.*

The cat is saying, "I'm *not* distancing! I'm a cat, darn it!"

Marriage goes best when at least one party can lighten up about differences. We all view reality through different filters depending on our class, culture, gender, birth order, genetic makeup, and unique family history. There are as many views of the truth as there are people who hold these views. There may also be differences in patterned ways that anxiety is managed (under stress, she seeks togetherness, he seeks distance).

Intimacy requires that we do not (a) get too nervous about differences, (b) operate as if we have the truth of the universe, or (c) equate closeness with sameness.

Keep in mind that differences don't mean one person is right and one person is wrong. Marriage requires us to stay emotionally connected to a partner who thinks, feels, and believes differently, without needing to change, fix, or convince the other person.

Strike When the Iron is Cold

No one thinks clearly in the midst of a tornado, so nothing is as important as getting a grip on your own intensity and calming down. Often, the worst time to speak out or open a difficult conversation is when you're feeling angry and intense.

Intensity breeds more intensity, only adding to the anxious emotional climate that blocked conversation to begin with. Also, keep in mind that your spouse is less likely to listen to criticism (even constructive criticism) when it's delivered in an intense or rat-a-tat-tat tone.

Apologize — or Otherwise Try to Repair a Disconnection

It's hard for many folks to apologize if they feel "over accused" or pushed to assume more than their fair share of the blame. As one man put it, "When my wife criticizes me, I don't want to apologize because I feel like I'm sticking my head on the chopping block. It doesn't feel equal. If I apologize, I'm agreeing with her that I'm the whole problem. And that's not true."

You can say, "I'm sorry for my part of the problem" even if you're secretly convinced that you're only 14 percent to blame. Marriage goes best when at least one person can apologize or find some other way to cut right through the nonproductive "whodunit" or "who started it" mentality. We know that the failure to *initiate* repair attempts — or the failure to *respond* to a partner's attempts to do so — is a flashing red light in marriage.

Warm Your Partner's Heart

During the courtship stage (or "Velcro Stage," as I call it) of relationships we know how to warm our partner's heart. We automatically focus on the positive and make our partner feel loved and valued and chosen. We may find our differences interesting or exciting and overlook the negative.

The longer people are married, the more this "selective attention" flips. Now we automatically pay attention to what we are critical about and that is what we notice and speak to. ("Why are you putting so much water in the pot for the pasta?" "Don't you know that's the wrong knife to cut a tomato?") We automatically fail to notice and comment on the positive. ("I loved the way you used humor to deal with your brother on the phone tonight.")

Try to focus on the positive even if you're feeling angry and resentful. Aim for a 5 to 1 ratio of positive to negative interactions (marriage expert John Gottman's formula for divorce busting). If you're feeling very angry with your partner, try the experiment just for one week and see what happens. Remember that no one will listen to criticism if there is not a surrounding climate of love and respect — or at least respect.

Practice Pure Listening

If our partner is saying something we don't want to hear, it takes courage to listen with an open heart, to give our full attention, and to not back away from asking, "Is there more you haven't told me?" Marriage is a good place to practice being a caring listener and a skilled questioner, without rushing in to offer advice, defend ourselves, or tell the other person how they should think and feel.

We naturally become defensive when our spouse begins to criticize us. We listen to refute or correct the inaccuracies, distortions, and exaggerations that are inevitably there. The challenge is to listen *only* to understand. Sometimes we need to decide in advance that we will try to listen differently — that *all* we will do in one particular conversation is listen and ask questions that will allow us to understand where the other person is coming from. We can save our defense for a future conversation.

To listen with an open heart and full emotional presence with the single goal of understanding your partner's pain, anger, or unhappiness is a spiritual exercise, in the truest sense of the word.

Stay Self-Focused (As Opposed to Focusing on Your Spouse)
When people come to see me for marital therapy, they are secretly hoping that I will fix or change their partner. But change will not happen until at least one person takes his or her blaming or worried focus off their spouse and puts it back on himself or herself.

Self-focus is not the same as self-blame. Rather, it means that we put our energy into observing, clarifying, and changing our own part in relationship patterns (we can only change ourselves) rather than trying to change, control, interpret, diagnose, or criticize the other party.

Part II: MOVING TOWARD A STRONG VOICE

Calm things down, warm things up, bite your tongue, appreciate differences, listen with an open heart...

This good advice can lead to a downward spiral, if we don't also work on having a bold and courageous voice. It doesn't help to be too good for our own good — to make excuses for a partner's unacceptable behavior or to tolerate behavior that is too costly to our own self.

All marriages require compromise and give-and-take, but the problem occurs when one person does far more than their 50 percent share of giving in and going along. We may adapt to unfair circumstances, or sacrifice too much of the self in marriage, despite the enormous long-term toll of making such accommodation.

While women have a long tradition of giving in and going along to preserve relationship harmony, men also lose their voice in marriage. The challenge of speaking wisely and well is an equal opportunity employer.

Establishing Your Bottom Line

Clarifying a bottom line in marriage is easy in theory and difficult in practice. It's not an exaggeration to say that for most couples, it's the work of at least one lifetime.

Strengthening our voice, and learning how to take a bottom-line position, when necessary, requires us to work on all of the following:

1. We can talk openly about things that are important to us.

2. We can define our values, beliefs, convictions, and principles and keep our own behavior in the marriage congruent with them.

3. We can take a clear position on where we stand on important emotional issues.

4. We can define the limits of what is acceptable and tolerable to us in a relationship.

5. We can define the limits of what we can comfortably do or give.

A true bottom-line position is not a threat or a reactive position fueled by anger ("Damn it! If you do that one more time, I'm leaving!"). It is not an expression of desperation or a last-ditch attempt to force a partner to shape up. It is not a mixed message, where our words say one thing ("I can't continue to take this") and our behavior says another (we continue to take it).

Instead, a bottom-line position evolves from a focus on the self, from a deeply felt awareness — which one can't fake, pretend, or borrow — of what we need and feel entitled to, and the limits of our tolerance.

We clarify a bottom line, not primarily to change or control the other person (although the wish to do so may certainly be there), but rather to preserve the dignity, integrity, and well-being of the self.

Everyone is different and there is no right bottom line for every person. But if we have no bottom line on important issues, our marriage — and our sense of self-worth — will spiral downward.

A Personal Example

One needn't clarify a bottom-line position in heavy, somber tones, nor need the issue be a big one. Here's an example:

There was a time when I was working too hard, traveling too much, and feeling overly responsible for breadwinning. I got grouchy about it and took jabs at my husband, Steve. To his credit, he let me know that he wasn't going to listen to my putting him down for not working enough hours to suit me.

When I "started in on him," as he put it, he'd lift his hand and say, "Stop. I don't want you to talk to me in that tone of voice." If I didn't stop or change my tone, Steve would end the conversation right then and there. He'd say, "I don't want to be criticized and I won't be talked to that way." Depending on his mood, he'd make his point with great maturity and lightness or great immaturity. Either way, he had a clear bottom line about what sort of conversations he wouldn't participate in.

Steve was not stonewalling me or ruling this (or any other) subject off limits. He expressed a willingness to sit down with me and look at both of our work schedules. He was clear that he was available for a conversation on any subject. He insisted only that I approach him as if he were a collaborative partner and not a big screw-up. That was his bottom line.

Steve and I don't resolve every difficult issue by taking a bottom-line position with each other about what we can or can't live with. Over the decades, we've been locked into some rather dramatic, non-productive fights where each of us keeps doing more of the same. But lightness and humor usually get us through both the small disagreements and the difficult impasses. When they don't, we find some other way of negotiating or tolerating our differences.

That said, we both know there is a line we can't cross, that there are certain behaviors the other won't tolerate over time. Even when it's not spelled out in words, couples know each other's bottom line, just like kids know what they can and can't get away with. And like a kid, a partner may keep pushing the limits until the other person says, "Enough!" and really means it. That place is our bottom line.

We need to know how and when to clarify a bottom-line position in every relationship we are in, but it is most difficult in marriage. My book, *The Dance of Connection*, will help you with this challenge when you're stuck in silence on the one hand, or nagging and complaining on the other, and your brain turns to mush, which it will.

Part III: THE DANCE OF MARRIAGE

The older I get, the more humble I am about marriage. The novelist Mary Karr defined a dysfunctional family as any family with more than one person in it. Ditto for marriage.

I always remind my readers that even the best marriages get stuck in too much distance, too much intensity, and too much pain. The automatic tendency toward fight or flight is hardwired in us, and marriage is a lightning rod that absorbs anxiety and intensity from every source. When stress is high enough, or lasts long enough, even the most mature, loving couples will get stuck in silence and distance (*flight* response) and/or conflict and blaming (*fight* response).

In case you haven't noticed, anxiety and stress will always be with us. And just because the universe sends you one gigantic stress, it doesn't mean that it won't hit you with others while you're down. So your mother's health is deteriorating, your dog dies, your son drops out of drug treatment, and your husband is laid off — all in the same year.

Because life is one thing after another, it's normal for married folks to yo-yo back and forth between distance and blame. But "normal" doesn't mean it's good for us — it just means it's the norm. You can expect it. If you aspire to have a remarkable marriage, free from entrenched distance and blame, you need to work on at least a few of the challenges I've laid out for you in this chapter.

My advice may look simple, but it is difficult to make a change and especially challenging to maintain it over time. To do so, you will need to have:

✤ *Goodwill and a genuine wish to have a better marriage.*

✤ *A relentless focus on the self. (This does not mean self-blame, but rather the capacity to observe and change your own steps in a pattern that is bringing you pain.)*

✤ *A willingness to engage in bold acts of change, and to stay on course over time.*

✤ *A willingness to practice, practice, practice.*

There is nothing worth doing that doesn't require practice, and having a good marriage is one of them. One can practice choosing happiness over the need to be right or to always win an argument. One can practice playfulness, generosity, and openness. One can practice having both a strong voice and a light touch. One can practice calming things down and warming them up even when the other person is being a big jerk.

If you're in a marriage now, you can use it as a laboratory to engage in creative acts of change, and observe the results of your own experiment. Start small and choose one thing from this chapter that you can do differently, and then maintain the change over time.

You may be tired of doing all the emotional work in your marriage, but if you want a better marriage, you are the only person you can control. And if you want a recipe for divorce, just wait for the other person to change first. The good news is that if you change your own steps, the old dance can't continue in the same way.

Recommended reading:
Books by Harriet Lerner

The Dance of Anger: A Woman's Guide to Changing the Patterns of Intimate Relationships

The Dance of Intimacy: A Woman's Guide to Courageous Acts of Change in Key Relationships

The Dance of Connection: How to Talk to Someone When You're Mad, Hurt, Scared, Frustrated, Insulted, Betrayed, or Desperate

The Mother Dance: How Children Change Your Life
(For stresses after kids come along or stepfamilies are formed)

(All published by Harper Paperbacks)

We Love Each Other But...Simple Secrets to Strengthen Your Relationship and Make Love Last by Dr. Ellen F. Wachtel (St. Martin's Griffin)

Also recommended:
Couples workshops and retreats with John Gottman, Ph.D., The Gottman Institute

JUDITH S. WALLERSTEIN, PH.D., is an internationally recognized authority on marriage. In 1980, she founded the Judith Wallerstein Center for the Family in Transition, in Marin County, California, a major center for research, education, and counseling for families in separation, divorce, and remarriage. Findings from her groundbreaking investigations have been widely published in scientific journals and such bestselling books as *The Good Marriage*, *The Unexpected Legacy of Divorce*, and *Second Chances*. Dr. Wallerstein has received awards from both the American Psychological Association and the American Bar Association.

SANDRA BLAKESLEE is a renowned science writer who was the co-author on Judith Wallerstein's landmark books *The Good Marriage*, *The Unexpected Legacy of Divorce*, and *Second Chances*. She is also the author, with her son Matthew, of *The Body Has a Mind of Its Own*, which was hailed as one of the "top five science books of 2007" by the *Washington Post*. Her work has been praised by Daniel Goleman, Larry Dossey, William Safire, *Psychology Today*, and *Nature*.

HAPPY MARRIAGES: DO THEY EXIST?

Judith S. Wallerstein, Ph.D. & Sandra Blakeslee

As a psychologist who has been studying the American family for most of my professional life, I have observed many changes in relationships between men and women and in society's attitudes about marriage and children. In 1980 I founded a large research and clinical center in the San Francisco Bay Area, where my colleagues and I have seen thousands of men, women, and children from families going through first or second divorces. Presently I am conducting a twenty-five-year follow-up of sixty couples who underwent divorce in 1971, with an emphasis on the lives of their 131 children, who are now grown and involved in their own marriages and divorces.

These young men and women, whom I have been interviewing at regular intervals as part of the longest study ever done on divorce, provide unique insights into its long-term effects on the American family. I have seen a great many children who, ten and fifteen years after their parents' divorce, are still struggling with unhappiness. On the threshold of adulthood, they are still in the shadow of that event. I am poignantly aware of how unfamiliar these children are with the kinds of relationships that exist in a happy family. Many tell me that they have never seen a good marriage.

I'm also concerned about the many men and women who remain lonely and sad years after a divorce. I'm doubly worried about the high divorce rate in second marriages with children, which compounds the suffering for everyone. I am sometimes criticized for being overly pessimistic about the long-term effects of divorce, but observations are drawn from the real world. Only if you see the children and parents of divorce day in and day out can you understand what the statistics mean in human terms.

I want to make it clear that I am not against divorce. I am deeply aware of how wretched a bad marriage can be and of the need for the remedy of divorce. But divorce by itself does not improve the institution of marriage. Some people learn from sad experience to choose more carefully the second time around. Others do not. Many never get a true second chance.

In the past twenty years, marriage in America has undergone a profound, irrevocable transformation, driven by changes in women's roles and the heightened expectations of both men and women. Without realizing it, we have crossed a marital Rubicon. For the first time in our history, the decision to stay married is purely voluntary. Anyone can choose to leave at any time — and everyone knows it, including the children. There used to be only two legal routes out of marriage — adultery and abandonment. Today one partner simply has to say, for whatever reason, "I want out." Divorce is as simple as a trip to the nearest courthouse.

Each year two million adults and a million children in this country are newly affected by divorce. One in two American marriages ends in divorce, and one in three children can expect to experience their parents' divorce. This situation has powerful ripple effects that touch us all. The sense that relationships are unstable affects the family next door, the people down the block, the other children in the classroom. Feelings of intense anxiety about marriage permeate the consciousness of all young men and women on the threshold of adulthood. At every wedding the guests wonder, privately, will this marriage last? The bride and groom themselves may question why they should marry, since it's likely to break up.

To understand how our social fabric has been transformed, think of marriage as an institution acted upon by centripetal forces pulling inward and centrifugal forces pulling outward. In times past the centripetal forces — law, tradition, religion, parental influence — exceeded those that could pull a marriage apart, such as infidelity, abuse, financial disaster, failed expectations, or the lure of the frontier. The weakened centripetal forces no longer exceed those that tug marriages apart.

In today's marriages, in which people work long hours, travel extensively, and juggle careers with family, more forces tug at the relationship than ever before. Modern marriages are battered by the demands of her workplace as well as his, by changing community values, by anxiety about making ends meet each month, by geographical moves, by unemployment and recession, by the vicissitudes of child care, and by a host of other issues.

Marriage counselors like to tell their clients that there are at least six people in every marital bed — the couple and both sets of parents. I'm here to say that a crazy quilt of conflicting personal values and shifting social attitudes is also in that bed. The confusion over roles and the indifference of the community to long-term conjugal relationships are there, as are the legacies of a self-absorbed, me-first, feminist-do-or-die, male-backlash society. The ease of divorce and changing attitudes about permanence of marriage have themselves become centrifugal forces.

Our great unacknowledged fear is that these potent outside forces will overwhelm the human commitment that marriage demands and that marriage as a lasting institution will cease for most people. We are left with a crushing anxiety about the future of marriage and about the men and women within it.

My study of divorce has inevitably led me to think deeply about marriage. Just as people who work with the dying worry about death, those of us who work with troubled marriages are constantly forced to look at our own relationships. So I have carefully taken note of my marriage and those of my grown children. As our fiftieth wedding anniversary approaches, I have thought long and hard about what my husband and I have done to protect our marriage. Why have we been able to love each other for so many years? Did we begin differently from those who divorced? Did we handle crises differently? Or were we just lucky? What have I learned that I can pass on to my children and my grandchildren?

I certainly have not been happy all through each year of my marriage. There have been good times and bad, angry and joyful moments, times of ecstasy and times of quiet contentment. But I would never trade my husband, Robert, for another man. I would not swap my marriage for any other. This does not mean that I find other men unattractive, but there is all the difference in the world between a passing fancy and a life plan. For me, there has always been only one life plan, the one I have lived with my husband. Buy why is this so? What makes some marriages work while others fail?

An acquaintance of mine — a highly regarded psychologist who has done extensive marriage counseling — called me when she became engaged. She said, "I want to spend several hours with you, drawing on your experience. My fiancé is several years older than I am and has been through one divorce. He's afraid of another failure. I'm thirty-eight years old and have for many years been frightened of marriage. What wisdom do you have for me based on your own marriage, which has always looked so ideal to me, and also based on your many years of work with divorce? Help me anticipate what lies ahead for Jim and me, so I can be prepared."

Her request intrigued me. What wisdom did she seek? She did not want shortcuts or hints but a realistic vision that could guide their efforts in building a successful marriage.

Not long after her call I decided to design a qualitative study of fifty couples who had built lasting, happy marriages, couples who had confronted the same obstacles, crises, and temptations as everyone else and had overcome them. As I began setting up the study, I drew up a list of questions that would guide my inquiry. Are the people in good marriages different from the men and women whose marriages fall apart? Are there common ideas, ways of dealing with the inevitable crises? What can we learn about selecting a partner, about sex, the stresses of the workplace, infidelity, the arrival of a baby or of adolescence, coping with midlife, aging, and retirement? What is happy in a marriage when people are in their twenties, thirties, forties, or fifties, and when they reach retirement? What are the central themes at each life stage? What makes men happy? What makes women happy? What does each spouse value in one another? What do they regard as the glue of the marriage?

From the beginning I was aware of the limitations of this kind of research, including the risk that it would attract vulnerable couples seeking a stamp of approval on their marriage, as well as the risks of selection bias, reliance on volunteers, and the small size of the sample. But I felt that these limitations were far outweighed by the potential understanding to be gained from exploring subjectively defined happiness in marriage. I planned to interview all of the individuals separately and each couple together over a two-year period.

Although fifty couples may seem too small a number from which to make sweeping conclusions about marriage, my conclusions are not meant to explain all there is to know about this subject. My intentions are much more modest. I have looked for commonalities as well as individual differences, hoping to find patterns on which to build general hypotheses. To me this is a fertile method of inquiry, but I should emphasize that I regard this as a pilot study. Further investigation would include more subjects and greater ethnic, geographic, and economic diversity, as well as homosexual couples.

The couples I studied, all of whom lived in northern California, were predominantly white, middle-class, and well educated. They do not represent the entire country and were not selected as typical. In a country as heterogeneous as ours, finding "typical" couples has limited value; the payoff comes from understanding different subgroups within the whole. The fifty couples represent a "first cut" within a particular socioeconomic group — but a group that is influential in setting social and cultural trends for the nation. Californians, who make up a sixth of the country's population, are more likely than other Americans to be distant from their families of origin and regions of birth — circumstances that are increasingly the norm in our highly mobile society.

The sample divided almost evenly among people who had married in the 1950s, 1960s, 1970s, and early 1980s. This provided a panoramic look at the changes that have overtaken marriage in the last four decades: the sexual revolution, the women's movement, the rise of dual-career couples.

I recruited the fifty couples by casting a wide net into the community, starting with the group of women who had heard my earliest thoughts on the study. For a while, whenever I spoke to professional groups, schools, social clubs, or other organizations, I requested as my fee the names of couples willing to participate in the marriage project. I found others with the help of my graduate students in the Department of Social Welfare at the University of California at Berkeley. These couples were younger and less affluent than the others in the study, and they had young children.

My criteria were straightforward. Both husband and wife had to consider their marriage a happy one. They had to have been married at least nine years, because the number of divorces peaks in the early years, and I wanted my subjects to be past that danger point. The shortest marriage studied was ten years, the longest forty years. The participants had to agree to lengthy interviews. I asked to see each spouse separately and then together in interviews that often lasted up to three hours each. Most people were interviewed at home, and a few at their place of work. I wanted to observe them in the surroundings they had created.

Although I had hoped to study only first marriages, it soon became clear that that was too limiting, so I included second marriages with children. The couple had to have produced children by the marriage, except in remarriages in which each partner brought at least one child from a previous marriage. I included children because all of my professional work has focused on families and because married couples without children either by choice or incapacity are psychologically and socially very different from those with children over the course of their lives. In some cases I met with children, and in a few instances I interviewed or played with them.

All of the participants understood that the questions and answers were on the record, that I could use all dialogue and family histories in this book, but that I would fully disguise their identities — not simply their names but their occupations and aspects of their surroundings. No one was paid; their only reward was in helping other people learn about good marriages. I was pleased at how open these people were — at how completely they trusted me. Because I promised full confidentiality, I was often privy to information that even the person's spouse did not have.

One very important goal of the study was to find out what people in these marriages meant by "happy." To what did they attribute their happiness? Were they happy from the start, and if not, what made the difference? I've always believed firmly that in a great many areas of life, especially in the realm of human relationships, ordinary people know a lot more than the experts. One of the major mistakes of my field is that we don't learn from people's expertise: we ask questions, but we don't listen to their wisdom.

Many years of working with divorcing couples have taught me how little one can tell about a marriage from the outside. Consider how surprised everyone is when the picture-book couple next door files for divorce. The interior does not match the façade. "Our family represents to some people a Camelot, when they view it from the outside," one woman told me. "Even those who know us don't see the nitty-gritty that every marriage goes through. But he and I know it. And our children do, now that they're grown." The problem, then, is how to gain entry into the inner sanctum of a marriage and not be misled by the front door.

I began each interview by asking, "Tell me what's good about this marriage." My second question was, "What's disappointing about your marriage?" This opening allowed each person to start wherever she or he was comfortable. More important, it gave my subjects no clues about what I might want to hear, and it anchored the discussion to the reality that all relationships are a mixture of good and less good elements.

I asked many questions about each person's parents, siblings, and other significant figures and about the major events of early life. I was interested in their view of the parents' marriage and their own relationship with each parent. I asked about experiences in adolescence and young adult life, including early sexual relationships, the steps that led to the marriage, and any misgivings they had had. I tried to elicit a full history of all domains of the marriage, including conflict, sex, extramarital relationships, household routines, work experience, friends, extended family,

crises, including deaths, and of course, the children. My intent
was to understand their life experience prior to the marriage, the
factors that had brought them together, and the changes that had
occurred during the marriage. I was also interested in fantasies,
roads not taken, and wishes that remained unfulfilled. Finally, I
wanted to know their perspective on their past and any advice
they had for others.

These couples spoke of their love for and friendship with each other
and of the pleasures and frustrations of parenting. They talked about
sex and passion, commitment and shared values. They described
stormy conflicts and long-standing differences. They recounted
their childhood histories and the relationships in their original
families. They talked about their first reactions to each other and to
each other's family and about their decision to marry. They made
it clear that they were not happy all the time. Many admitted that
at times they wanted out. Some confessed that on occasion they
felt they had made a mistake. But each person felt strongly that
on balance their marriage had a goodness of fit in needs, wishes,
and expectations. Although everyone was reluctant to define love,
they spoke movingly, often lyrically, about how much they valued,
respected, and enjoyed the other person and how appreciative they
were of the other's responsiveness to their needs.

They stressed different aspects of the relationship. Some said that
their marriage had given them a sense of continuity and of hope for
the future. One thirty-eight-year-old man said, "We share a vision

about how our lives will unfold — like when we're seventy, our kids will be good and responsible people who care about the world and other people."

Others emphasized the security that marriage afforded. One woman said, "I feel safer in this marriage than I have ever felt in any other place in my life." Another said, "I knew we would go through forty years of ups and downs, but it would be absolutely inconceivable to me that we wouldn't make it to the end of our lives. And I think that he feels that way too. It gives you this incredible feeling of safety and comfort, so that you don't have to ask those wrenching questions over and over again. And I know that is at the core of our sense of security in an insecure world."

Happy marriages are not carefree. There are good times and bad times, and certainly partners may face serious crises together or separately. Happily married husbands and wives get depressed, fight, lose jobs, struggle with the demands of the workplace and the crises of infants and teenagers, and confront sexual problems. They cry and yell and get frustrated. They come from sad, abusive, neglectful backgrounds as well as from more stable families; all marriages are haunted by ghosts from the past.

Every good marriage must adapt to developmental changes in each partner, bending and yielding to the redefinitions that all men and women go through. It must expand to accommodate children, close ranks when the children leave home, and metamorphose at retirement. But somehow, for reasons that are critically important and that I explore here, these people have stayed married despite the *Sturm und Drang* of modern life. They feel, and say with conviction, that the marriage will last. After ten, twenty, thirty, or more years of being together, they regard the marriage with contentment and feel confident about its survival.

By observing these couples, I learned how much marriage has changed over the past decades. The changes are reflected in the different expectations and experiences of the men and women who married in each of the decades from the fifties to the early eighties. A particularly striking change is in the sexual experiences of women prior to marriage and in the woman's role within the marriage. All of the women who married in the fifties were either virgins or pregnant at the wedding, whereas none of those who married during the early eighties were virgins. Some had had sexual experiences with many lovers, beginning when they were fifteen. The rise of dual-career families and the increased anxiety about divorce are also seen in the experiences of those couples.

Marriage is an ever-changing relationship, and it must be examined at several points along the way. A snapshot cannot substitute for a portrait of marriage over time. Two years after the first interview with each couple, I contacted them again, and everyone agreed to a second interview. In that short time, a period of economic recession, all kinds of changes had occurred. People were really worried about making ends meet. Some middle-aged husbands had lost jobs that they could never hope to match. One man got the job he'd wanted his whole life and had moved his family to London.

The shock waves of adolescence had rocked many families. Some children won prizes; one boy was expelled from school for smoking marijuana. In one family the child of a former marriage turned up without warning. There had been unexpected promotions, accidents (including one head-on collision on the Golden Gate Bridge in which three family members were seriously hurt), and life-threatening illnesses. Several grandparents had died. In short, a lot of life had happened. But no couple had divorced.

Early in this century Carl Jung told us that marriage is the most complex of human relationships. Today marriage is more fragile than ever. But I am committed to the view that if a man and woman begin their marriage with a healthy respect for its complexity, they stand a much greater chance of success. If they can grasp the richly nuanced, subtle needs that people bring from their childhood experiences and can understand how the past connects with the present, they can build mutual understanding and love based on true intimacy. If they can see how each domain of marriage connects with every other — especially how their sex life affects every aspect of their relationship — and if they can acknowledge the central conflicts in all marriages and the importance of friendship and nurturance in muting those conflicts, they will be well on their way toward building an enduring relationship. Finally, if they can appreciate the myriad ways that people grow and change through the years and realize that a happy, lasting marriage is challenged and rebuilt every day, then they will have acquired the only map there is for a successful lifetime journey together.

JOHN GRAY, PH.D., is the bestselling relationship author of all time. He is the author of sixteen bestselling books including *Men Are from Mars, Women Are from Venus,* one of the most popular books of the last decade. In the past fifteen years, over 40 million Mars Venus books have been sold in over forty-five languages throughout the world. Dr. Gray has appeared on *The Oprah Winfrey Show, The Today Show, CBS Morning Show, Good Morning America, The Early Show,* and *The View,* and he has been profiled in *Newsweek, Time, Forbes, USA Today, People,* and numerous other publications. He is a member of the Distinguished Advisory Board of the International Association of Marriage and Family Counselors. In 2001 he received the Smart Marriages Impact Award.

Dance Steps for Lasting Intimacy

John Gray, Ph.D.

I always enjoy watching older couples dance. They seem so happy together. They know just what to do, he has all the moves down, and she trusts him to lead her exactly where she wants to go. She melts into his arms and he holds her charmingly and confidently. This trust and confidence can only come with years of practice.

When couples start out in love, they are always willing to do whatever it takes to make the relationship work. The problem is that the dance steps that worked for past generations don't work today. The music has changed, and new steps are required. Without an awareness of these new advanced skills, it is inevitable that the special light of love we feel in the beginning will grow dimmer.

When a man is skilled in loving a woman, there is no question that his love can sweep her off her feet. In a similar way, a woman's love can help plant a man's feet firmly on the ground. By learning new skills to express her love, she can be a mirror to help him see and feel his greatness. She can be a motivating force that helps him succeed in expressing his most competent and loving self.

The Well-Earned Gift of Love

The support I have experienced through my wife's gentle and sometimes fierce love for me has dramatically influenced my ability to relax and feel good about myself. It has allowed the real and loving person to come out of me.

For example, instead of being critical when I would forget things, she was accepting and patient. This was the gentle love. But instead of giving up and doing things for herself without my help, she persisted in a nondemanding way. This was her fierce love. She didn't give up like so many women do. She kept on practicing the dance steps.

Although Bonnie's love is a gift that I have earned, it is also given freely. Through her willingness to "pause and postpone" her immediate needs, "prepare me" to listen and respond to her requests, and "persist" in asking for my support in a nondemanding way, I gradually discovered how important love was and how to get it.

The growth we have experienced together has been the result of hard work. Now it is much easier. Life always has its difficult challenges, but with new skills for relating we are able to grow closer instead of farther apart in our journey together. We are able to support each other in our ongoing process of living, growing, and sharing ourselves in the world.

As I have focused on developing my masculine side to improve communication by learning to duck, dodge, disarm, and deliver, she has focused on developing her female side to assist me in being successful in fulfilling her. Through her learning to pause, prepare, postpone, and persist, it has made a world of difference.

Although neither of us is perfect in these skills, each day we get better. They are no longer difficult to practice because we know they work, and we know how painful it is when we don't use them. Sometimes she is the more supportive, while at other times she has little to give. Even when both of us are empty, just knowing how to start giving again to get the support we need is a tremendous source of strength.

When I am in my cave and Bonnie is not getting what she needs, instead of panicking or feeling responsible, she knows how to pause and give me space. She practices preparing me to do more by asking for support in easy ways and then appreciating me.

Instead of trying to change me or improve the relationship, she focuses on using her feminine skills to give me space and gradually draw me out of the cave with her patient love.

Two Steps Forward and Then Back Again

Just like dance partners, when a woman takes two steps back, the man can take two steps forward. When he takes two steps back, she can take two steps forward. This give-and-take is the basic rhythm of relationships.

At other times, they both pull back and then come back together. Every relationship has those times when both partners have little to give and so they pull back to recharge.

While dancing, a woman gracefully swings into the man's arms, then spins away. In a successful relationship, this same pattern is expressed. A woman is happy to see her partner, she moves into his arms, and then after pausing and preparing him, she spins out of his arms, and shares her feelings in a circular manner.

At other times, he will hold her in his arms as she swings back and dips. In a similar way, as a woman shares her feelings she may dip. With his sympathetic support she is able to go almost all the way down to the dance floor and then experience the joy of coming back up.

In dance, a woman naturally spins around while the man stays steady. In a similar manner, when a woman can share her feelings without a man reacting with his, she can feel heard. Certainly, there are also times when they both spin, but as in dance they need to pull away to do the movement before again making contact.

While dancing, a man gets to feel his sense of independence and autonomy by leading, and a woman gets to feel her need for cooperation and relationship through supporting him as he supports her in the moves she wants to make.

The Care and Feeding of Partnerships

In our journey we must remember to nurture and respect our differences. Differences create passion. We start relationships because we are drawn to another person who is different but complements us.

In the beginning, Bonnie and I had no idea how different we were. We were so focused on the ways in which we were similar. We were both very spiritual, we both enjoyed sex, we both liked to go for walks, we both liked tennis, we both liked movies, we had many friends in common, we were both easygoing, we were both interested in psychology. The list of commonalities was delightfully long.

Once we were married, we began to notice the differences. I was detached, she was emotional. I was goal oriented, she was relationship oriented. She liked discussing problems, I wanted to solve or postpone them. Besides these and other standard gender differences that create the inherent attraction between the sexes, there were many other differences as well that are not necessarily gender based.

She liked the bedroom temperature cool, and I liked it warm. She liked antiques, and I liked high-tech and modern. She liked to balance her checkbook to the last penny, and I would round it off and get a vague running total in my mind. She liked to get up early, and I liked to stay up late. She liked eating at home, and I liked going out. She drove the speed limit, and I liked to drive fast. She liked to save money, and I liked to spend it. She made decisions slowly, and I liked to make them fast. She held on to old relationships, and I quickly moved on. I have big ambitions, and she is quite content with her life the way it is. I like electric gadgets, and she likes the garden and other "real" things of the earth. She likes to visit museums, and I like elegant hotels. I like new, modern homes, and she likes older, more charming homes. I like views with a vista, and she likes being in the woods.

Although each of these differences creates a possible conflict, they also create the opportunity to grow together as well. In relationships, we are generally attracted to a person with certain qualities that, in a sense, are either dormant within or yet to come out of us. When we are one way and our partner is another way, we are instinctively attracted to them to help us find balance with ourselves. Finding this balance creates passion and attraction.

After about a year of being married, I confronted my first big challenge relating to our differences. I wanted to buy a larger-screen TV. I love new technology and gadgets. Bonnie wasn't in favor of the idea. She said that she didn't like the idea of having to see it looming in the living room every day.

This was a very difficult moment for me. I began to feel that to make her happy, I had to give up something that would make me happy. At that point I was just beginning to understand how we could resolve our differences by working out a win/win solution.

Internally, I was furious. All kinds of buttons were being pushed, but I contained myself by remaining focused on finding a solution. As long as I kept thinking that we could both somehow get what we wanted, the frustration did not turn to anger at her.

"I want to respect your wishes," I finally told her. "And I really want to get a bigger TV. I've waited a long time to be able to afford one. I also really want you to have a beautiful home. What do you think we can do?"

Bonnie answered, "I wouldn't mind a big TV if it was in a cabinet that closed in the front. Then when you weren't watching it, I could close it and not always have to see it."

I immediately said great, and we went together to buy a cabinet. I thought it was going to be an easy solution. We soon found we had completely different tastes in furniture.

The Win/Win Solution

The cabinet I picked out was high-tech and would hold all my stereo equipment. The cabinet she wanted had glass-backed shelves with lights for displaying china and crystals, but it didn't have a big enough space for the TV that I wanted.

For weeks we looked for something that would accommodate our differing needs. During this process, I felt like I wanted to explode, but I did everything I could to contain my frustration. It was a very difficult time. I thought that she was so stubborn and resistant, and I became very judgmental of her. In my darkest moments I thought, I'm getting a divorce!

Hindsight helps us to see how we tend to blow things out of proportion. Although I thought she was being stubborn, I was being just as stubborn. I wanted my big-screen TV, and she wanted it covered. I wanted a cabinet to hold my stereo, and she wanted something to hold her crystal and beautiful things.

We teetered on the brink of hating each other, and then came the day when we finally found a cabinet we both agreed on. It was a miracle. Except that we had to wait another three months for it to be shipped to us. The whole ordeal couldn't have been more frustrating, but once the cabinet arrived, we were both very satisfied with it.

Building Relationship Muscles

What we ended up getting together was much better than what I would have gotten if I'd gone shopping on my own. By stretching myself to include and respect Bonnie's tastes and wishes, I had achieved an end result far greater than anything I alone could have created. Through exercising our patience and flexibility we were both able to strengthen our relationship.

This experience became a strong metaphor for all our future conflicts. I realized that even when it seemed that I could not get what I wanted, with persistence and a willingness to fulfill both our wishes, we would always end up with more. Although I didn't initially care much for the display shelves, I love and greatly appreciate them now. And Bonnie greatly enjoys the thirty-six-inch TV.

Once we had worked through this problem successfully, I realized that we were much closer than we had been before. Our trust level had gone up. The strength, patience, faith, and flexibility it took to find a win/win solution made other challenges much easier.

Partnership and Service to a Higher Purpose

Partnership is one of the secrets to creating a lasting and passionate relationship. To create a mutually fulfilling partnership, it is helpful to understand how men and women experience partnership differently.

A woman feels partnership when she and her partner are doing things together in a cooperative manner toward the same goal. There is no hierarchy or boss. They make all decisions together, sharing their input equally.

A man experiences partnership very differently. He likes to have his department, where he is in control, and he is happy for her to have her department, where she is in control. He doesn't want her telling him what to do, nor does he feel he has to be involved with what she is doing. Together, doing different jobs with different responsibilities, they are a partnership teaming up to get the job done.

With an awareness of this difference, both men and women can create the partnership they want. Using sexual intercourse as a metaphor, we can easily see the solution. In sex, a man leaves his world and enters hers. This brings them both great pleasure. Then, quite naturally, he pulls back into his world (or department), leaving her alone in her world (or department). Then again, back and forth, he moves in and out of her world. In a similar way, to create a win/win partnership, a couple can have more or less clear departments, and the man can occasionally move into hers and help her as an equal.

As he gets better and better at working and cooperating with her in her departments, then slowly but surely he will begin to invite her into his departments. Using this as a general guideline can be very helpful, particularly when couples work together.

For a partnership to thrive and not be self-serving, it must have a purpose beyond itself. For the passion to grow, partners must share a common interest and work toward that end.

We all come into this world with gifts to share and purposes to fulfill beyond our personal happiness. They may not be earth-shattering, but they are there. For a relationship to grow in love and passion, the love we share with another needs to be directed in some loftier way.

Having children is a natural fulfillment of this need. As a team, parents give to each other so that they can more successfully give to the children.

Once children grow up and leave home, couples need to find a new goal or purpose. When as a partnership we are serving the highest good of the family, community, or world, our love can continue to grow without limit.

The Power of Forgiveness

To fully open our hearts to each other and enjoy a lifetime of love, the most important skill of all is forgiveness. Forgiving your partner for their mistakes not only frees you to love again but allows you to forgive yourself for not being perfect.

When we don't forgive in one relationship, our love is, to various degrees, restricted in all our life relationships. We can still love others, but not as much. When a heart is blocked in one relationship, it beats more weakly in them all. Forgiving means letting go of hurt.

Forgiveness allows us to give our love again and helps us to open up both to give and also to receive love. When we are closed, we lose on two counts.

The more you love someone, the more *you* suffer when you don't forgive them. Many people are driven to suicide by the agonizing pain of not forgiving a loved one. The greatest pain we can ever feel is the pain of not loving someone we love.

This agony drives people mad and is responsible for all the violence and craziness in our world and in our relationships. It is this pain of holding back our love that moves many people to addictive behaviors, substance abuse, and random violence.

We stubbornly hold on to bitterness and resentment not because we are not loving, but because we do not know how to forgive. If we were not loving, then ceasing to love someone would not be painful at all. The more loving we are, the more painful it is to not forgive.

One of the country's leading marriage experts, TERRI ORBUCH, PH.D., known as "The Love Doctor,®" has a popular morning segment on relationships on WJBK Fox 2 News – Detroit. She has published over forty articles and has been quoted in such national publications as the *New York Times*, the *Boston Globe*, and *Reader's Digest*. She is the project director of the groundbreaking Early Years of Marriage Project (1986 – present), which is funded by the National Institutes of Health. Dr. Orbuch is the author of five relationship books, including *5 Simple Steps to Take Your Marriage from Good to Great*.

How to Have a Loving Marriage, Even with Less Money, Less Time, and More Stress

Terri Orbuch, Ph.D.

Maintaining a strong, loving marriage is a challenge even during the best of times. So when couples are stressed to the max by a sluggish economy that leaves them with too little time and money — and way too much stress — feeling the love and enjoying each other's company just gets a whole lot tougher.

Today's economy is in tatters, yet many of us find ourselves busier than ever. We spend more time trying to make ends meet — and less time trying to keep our marriage strong and committed. We're always on the go and working longer hours for less money. We're worried about our jobs, our health, and our kids.

But my experience as a relationship expert, researcher, and therapist has shown me that even during these worst of times it is possible to forge a loving relationship. In fact, working on your relationship just may be the most important thing you do right now if you want to wake up next to your current partner when life as we know it returns to a less-crazed state.

> *When my wife landed a job to help make ends meet, I thought it was a great idea. But then we began to bicker about things like who should keep the house clean and who should take the kids to sports practice or dance classes . . . We were constantly tired and stressed. The passion evaporated from our marriage and I feared we'd be heading to divorce court unless things got back on track and fast.* — *John M.*

Sound familiar? Many of the couples I work with lose sight of the fact that they need to lean on each other at times like these — not butt heads over the tasks that are tearing them apart. I wouldn't blame you for thinking that it's inevitable that all of this external stress and pressure would break up marriages in record numbers. But you'd be wrong. It is extremely possible to have a loving marriage even when faced with less time, less money, and more stress!

The Science Behind Loving Marriages

In and around the greater Detroit area, I have a private practice as a marriage and family therapist; teach as a university professor; and direct a long-term research project on marriage at the University of Michigan, funded by the National Institutes of Health. Outside of my counseling office and university affiliations, I am known as The Love Doctor®, a nationally recognized relationship expert and author. And, after years of hands-on experience helping couples with their relationships, I have come up with a four-part prescription to soothe stress and resuscitate strained marriages. The best part is that this advice is based on science, rather than commonsense notions of what might create a loving marriage.

My long-term project on marriage is a landmark study. The project began in 1986 and it is the only study of its kind. I have been following 373 married couples for more than twenty-two years. With a team of highly trained researchers, I interviewed the couples at their homes multiple times. Previous research studies on marriage have relied either on couples seeking marital counseling or on volunteers recruited through advertising. The problem with studying these groups is that couples in counseling are likely to be experiencing more marital problems than the average, whereas volunteers may be more secure with their relationships. In contrast, I turned to couples who were applying for marriage licenses in order to obtain a diverse group of couples.

As I note in my book, *5 Simple Steps to Take Your Marriage from Good to Great* (Random House Publishing, 2009), it's not the big events that make couples unhappy. No, it's more likely the seemingly minor everyday challenges — your partner not seeming to notice you or listen to you, or appearing bored. By counseling and interviewing hundreds of couples, I've found it to be true that it is indeed the small annoyances and irritations that quite often lead to unhappiness and instability.

I, too, was surprised to find that the bigger blows like death, unemployment, or bankruptcy are not the greatest sources of marital strife or struggles. On the contrary, I have discovered that in times of great hardship, couples tend to lean on each other. When there is great stress coming from outside the marriage, most of us turn to our partners for relief, love, and support. Many of the couples in my study agree that today's tough times and life-changing challenges have brought them closer together.

The nation's divorce rate has actually decreased. Statistics show that during the mid-1980s nearly two out of three couples were doomed to divorce. The odds of staying married improved to about half in the mid-1990s. Today, as couples are faced with challenges that involve keeping a job and a roof over their heads, even fewer are opting out of a relationship. The most recent statistics show that the divorce rate today has dropped to as low as 45 percent. Telling numbers indeed!

> *My employer downsized and I lost my job and very nearly lost my home. If it hadn't been for my wife I don't know how I would have made it through this mess. Rather than turn to the bottle like I used to do as a bachelor, I found myself turning more and more to my wife for support and reassurance that things were going to be okay. We're still fighting to pay our bills but at least we aren't fighting with each other. I feel closer to her than ever and that makes me feel like a rich man!* — Gary R.

Focus on New Positive Elements
All marriages have their ups and downs. There is no perfect marriage. But findings from my long-term study show that what

keeps couples together and happy is just as important to address and recognize. It is the positive approach to healthy relationships and marriages. Instead of focusing on what is wrong in a marriage, it's also important to concentrate on what you can add to or include in your marriage to promote happiness and stability.

A mistake that many couples make — as do many couples' therapists, I might add — is that they focus on the negative. What's wrong with this marriage, they ask? How can we fix it? My years of therapeutic experience and scientific observation have led me to conclude that a very different — and perhaps opposite — approach works better. I have found that the most effective way to boost happiness, commitment, harmony, fun, and passion in a marriage that is basically sound is to add new elements to the marriage, and to focus on how to support and strengthen what's already working well. Contrary to popular belief, a fulfilling marriage doesn't require years of hard work. The simplest targeted actions can bring significant positive changes to a relationship.

My years of research have revealed there are four specific things you can do to keep your marriage loving and happy — even when annoying outside factors like less money, less time, and more stress chip away at your state of mind. The loving marriages in my long-term study have four important ingredients: *realistic expectations, reconnections with spouse, trust, and affective affirmation.*

Be Realistic

My research shows that frustration is the leading reason marriages are unhappy. When our real-life experiences don't match our expectations of what we think should happen, we feel frustration and stress. Then we become unhappy with our partner and our relationship. You should always have realistic expectations about marriage, relationships, and the opposite sex in general. Also, make sure you know your partner's specific expectations for a good relationship.

> *I guess I thought my wife would have the wisdom of a June Cleaver when it came to handling our kids . . . I got angry with her when she was as mystified as me, trying to deal with the problems that arose as our children got older. If I could go back, I'd trash everything I thought I knew about relationships and parenting, and instead work with my wife to be better parents and partners.* — *Jack C.*

It's time to be real folks. Don't believe everything you hear or see on TV. The happy marriages we adore on our favorite half-hour sitcoms (think the Huxtables or the Bradys) are the result of good writing, not actual real-life experiences. No one that I know has ever worked out a marital problem in thirty minutes (twenty-two minutes if you don't count the commercials)! It just doesn't happen here in the real world.

It is also important to identify the rules for your ideal relationship, as well as those of your partner. There are rules to everything, and relationships are no exception. Relationship rules are the expectations that you have for how a good relationship should work. We all have expectations for our partner (how he or she should behave or treat us) and for our relationship (how it should be now and how it should develop in the future). These rules vary from one person to another and often change depending on what is happening around you. Studies show that if your partner doesn't know your relationship rules or what you think a happy relationship looks like to you, you can become very frustrated or angry.

Let's imagine your partner assumes that happy couples share leisure time together and expects that you will spend time with him or her when you are not working. You, on the other hand, feel that in happy relationships, partners need to have their own hobbies, interests, and friends. The two of you disagree about your plans for leisure time. This difference is not a problem — but communication with each other is the key to happiness.

Do yourself a favor and make a list of your relationship rules or expectations. Then, share these expectations with your spouse and make sure she or he understands that these are important when it comes to how you think your relationship should work. Ask your partner to clearly explain to you the relationship rules that are important to her or him. Differences in expectations are fine — and predictable. The important thing is that you and your partner discover what each of you thinks is essential to a good relationship.

After you have shared your expectations with each other, be sure to *appreciate your differences* and *build on your similarities*. I encourage couples to have these joint discussions at least once a year. This is necessary because your rules may change depending on what is happening around you. For example, if you are feeling particularly insecure at work one month, you may need more affirmation and less criticism from your partner at home. On the other hand, if you are feeling secure and confident at work, you may be more able to handle criticism from your partner at home.

Reconnect and Recharge

Life got busier — there's no arguing that point. However, because life seems to like traveling in the fast lane, it is of the utmost importance that we occasionally hit the brakes and take time to reconnect and recharge our relationship. We all get caught up in work, family, and responsibilities. This daily grind pushes us to put our relationship on the back burner so we can douse one fire after another. If this sounds like you, you need to know that the biggest fire you must tend to right now is your flagging relationship. It's time to carve out some quality time with your partner.

Feeling frazzled or maybe overwhelmed by your busy life? Relax and take a deep breath. All relationships have those times when one or both partners are stressed for some reason. Really tense times in a relationship can either pull you and your mate apart or bring you closer together. Therefore, the key to a successful marriage is learning how to weather the hassles and pressures together.

Also, it's extremely important that you and your partner learn how to de-stress together. Taking the time to chill out with your partner will increase intimacy and closeness between the two of you — and that's something that can even boost your health.

Working out with my husband has brought us closer together. No matter how crazy my day is, I know that when Stan and I go for our walk or hit the gym together, things are going to feel much better — and I will lose a lot of the stress that has been weighing me down. — Carla J.

You might also want to find time to exercise together. A few good ways to relieve your frustrations and have some fun include walking, biking, and playing a sport together. Just be sure to leave your competitiveness on the sidelines! Your partner can motivate you to stay with your workout program or help get you off the couch when needed. But most importantly, research shows that the arousal hormones produced through exercise can make you more amorous and that can spice up your relationship.

You'll also want to get creative together! By creative, I mean doing things like cooking, pottery, art, listening to music, or even reading to one another. When done as a couple, these activities can be extremely relaxing. So go ahead and use your imagination to escape from the pressures and strains brought on by economic hardship.

Oh, and don't forget to laugh! Too often we get caught up in matters of financial security, the challenges of raising children, and the demands of our jobs. We forget that our marriage should also include loads of fun and happiness. Remind yourself to smile and laugh with your partner. Laughter reduces the level of your stress hormones. It also creates a positive feeling and a sense of connection between you and your partner. So have a bit of fun at a comedy club or stay home and rent a funny movie tonight.

A Matter of Trust

Trust is also an essential part of a good marriage. You need to trust your spouse. When you trust someone, you believe that person tells you the truth and that he or she wouldn't hurt or deceive you. For a loving relationship, it's important that you and your partner each feel a sense of trust. I recommend couples have regular "trust chats." What's a trust chat? It's simply a conversation that will hopefully give both of you a strong sense of shared values. During your trust chat, ask each other questions like, "What does commitment mean to you?" and "Is it acceptable to have secrets from one another?"

Studies show that if you trust your spouse, this reduces your inhibitions and worries and you are free to share feelings and dreams with each other. Once this sharing occurs, you also feel closer and more connected to your spouse. For a shot at a long-term happy marriage, you need to be able to trust others and you need to have a partner who is trustworthy.

I love the fact I can tell Donald everything and anything about my day — good or bad. I didn't have this type of trust in my first marriage and I am sure that's what led to my divorce. I don't expect Donald to be happy with everything I say, but I feel secure in knowing I can share my innermost feelings with my husband. It's an awesome thing! I always hated keeping things to myself. That was so stressful. — Leanne D.

In my long-term study of marriage, I asked the happiest couples to name their "most important" marriage expectation. A whopping 92 percent of the men and 96 percent of the women answered: "You should feel that your spouse would never hurt or deceive you!" Billy Joel sang about it, and I am here to echo his refrain: It's a matter of trust.

In my study, happy couples were also honest with each other. Yes, this means not lying. But it also means being forthcoming and open. You both need to feel that the relationship is a safe place where you can be vulnerable and fully present. That means bringing up personal, embarrassing, or even potentially contentious topics. So if you're overdrawn on your checking account or you're in danger of losing your job, you need to let your partner know. Any temporary embarrassment will vanish the moment your spouse wraps his or her arms around you and assures you that things will be all right.

Little Things Mean a Lot

The fourth and final part of maintaining a good marriage during even the most troubling times is: affirming and validating one another. I call this *affective affirmation*. Affective affirmation is the degree to which you feel noticed and made to feel special by your partner. When you feel like your partner affirms you often, you are happier in your marriage. Interestingly, this affective affirmation seems to be more important for men than women. Women tend to get this affirmation from people outside the marriage (think sisters, best friends, mother, children, and neighbors). Sadly, most men do not. Therefore, husbands rely on their wives to affirm and validate them.

My advice to both sexes: For a good, loving marriage — a union that can weather the worst of economic times — be sure to give your partner affective affirmation frequently. Whether your compliments are for their scrumptious cooking, super sense of humor, or amazing organizational skills, take notice of your mate's special talents and let her or him know how much you appreciate those talents! Partners who get too little affective affirmation can become resentful and sad. No one should feel that his or her wonderful qualities are going unnoticed or unappreciated.

The next time the evening news weighs heavily on your mind, turn off the television, seek out your husband or wife, and give him or her a big, heartfelt hug. You may not be able to control the stock market or the shuttering of yet another business, but you *can* control your relationship.

GAY HENDRICKS, PH.D., has served for more than thirty-five years as one of the major contributors to the fields of relationship transformation and body/mind therapies. Along with his wife, Dr. Kathlyn Hendricks, Dr. Gay Hendricks is the coauthor of many bestsellers, including *Conscious Loving: Spirit-Centered Relationships*. He is the author of thirty-two books, including *The Corporate Mystic*, *Conscious Living*, *Five Wishes*, and *The Big Leap*. Dr. Hendricks received his Ph.D. in counseling psychology from Stanford in 1974. After a twenty-one-year career as a professor at the University of Colorado, he founded The Hendricks Institute, which offers seminars in North America, Asia, and Europe.

How to Create a Conscious, Loving Marriage: The Seven Keys

Gay Hendricks, Ph.D.

As of this writing, my wife, Kathlyn, and I are celebrating our thirtieth year together. Early in our relationship, we set the intention of creating a marriage that ran on positive energy rather than the up-and-down fluctuations of negative and positive. We'd learned in earlier relationships that the repetitive cycles of get close/get into conflict/get close/get into conflict were taxing and tedious. It took us quite a few years, but as of now, it's been nearly fifteen years, for example, since either one of us has criticized or blamed the other one for anything. To live in a household where nary a critical word is spoken is a delicious thing indeed. I highly recommend it.

If you are drawn to create that kind of magic for yourself, here are the operating instructions, as clearly and simply as I can make them. Kathlyn and I have taught these principles and practices to more than 20,000 people in our live seminars, as well as to larger audiences on *Oprah* and other programs we've been on. As one of my mentors used to say about even the most powerful technique: they work, if you do. In other words, if you take the time to practice as well as understand the principles, you can make remarkable gains in the amount of love and intimacy you enjoy.

Ready? Let the journey begin:

THE FIRST PRINCIPLE

Relationships thrive when each partner commits to total union with the other person and total creative expression as an individual.

The First Practice

Make a heartfelt commitment to your partner that you're willing to go beyond all your ego-defenses to full unity. At the same time, make a commitment to going all the way with your own individual creative expression. Then observe the emergence of your defensive barriers every day. Communicate about them honestly, <u>but don't take them seriously</u>. In fact, ego-defenses disappear quickly when you turn them into play.

꙳

THE SECOND PRINCIPLE

Relationships thrive when each partner learns from every relationship interaction, especially the stressful ones, instead of running programmed defensive moves. Some popular defensive moves: criticizing, lying, sulking in silence, making noisy uproars, and numbing out with food, drink, smoke, TV, and other habit-forming drugs.

The Second Practice

Make a heartfelt commitment to learning something new from every relationship interaction. Notice your defensive moves as they emerge, and gradually transplant wondering and truth-speaking in place of defensiveness.

THE THIRD PRINCIPLE

Relationships thrive in a climate of absolute honesty — no hidden feelings or withheld truths. All feelings — anger, sadness, joy, fear, sexual attraction — are okay to discuss with the other person, and each person is able to listen, free of listening-filters such as listening-to-find-fault and listening-to-fix.

The Third Practice

Notice your feelings and thoughts, and speak about them to your partner. If there are things you've done or feelings you're afraid to talk about, make <u>sure</u> to speak about those to your partner. Get familiar with your habitual listening-filters, and practice summarizing what the other person is saying, with no distortion, and acknowledging the feelings embedded in communication.

THE FOURTH PRINCIPLE

Relationships thrive when people keep their agreements impeccably. It doesn't matter whether an agreement seems trivial ("Sorry, honey, but I forgot to take the trash out") or significant ("Sorry, honey, but I slept with your twin sister and the maid of honor the night before our wedding"). There is no such thing as a minor lapse of integrity.

The Fourth Practice
Monitor each agreement you make very carefully, making sure you want to make it in the first place. Once you make an agreement, fulfill it impeccably or change it consciously by communicating with the relevant person.

✦

THE FIFTH PRINCIPLE
People thrive in a climate of 100 percent accountability, where nobody blames or claims victim status. One hundred percent accountability is the shift from "I was wronged" to "I take full responsibility for events occurring the way they did." From this empowered position, problems can be solved quickly, because time and energy are not squandered in a fruitless attempt to find fault.

The Fifth Practice
In any situation, claim responsibility for having created it the way it occurred. Wonder about how and why you might have wanted it to occur that way. Speak in empowered language rather than victim language ("I choose to go to the dentist" rather than "I have to go to the dentist," "I take responsibility for eating so that I have a healthy body" rather than "Why did you buy that huge bucket of buttered popcorn? You know I can't resist it.").

✦

THE SIXTH PRINCIPLE
Relationships flourish when partners appreciate each other

liberally. People grow more beautiful through our appreciation of them. Relationships take a quantum leap when each partner practices appreciation of the other person as a daily art form.

The Sixth Practice

Invent new ways to appreciate the other person every day, and speak appreciations frequently. Live inside questions such as, "What is my partner's true essence and how can I invite it forth?" And "What could I appreciate about my partner at this moment?"

THE SEVENTH PRINCIPLE

Everything can be resolved with willingness and love. Love is the ultimate healer and liberator, because only love is vast enough to embrace its opposite. In other words, you can love yourself even when you hate yourself, and the hate will melt in the larger presence of love. Whatever emerges in a close relationship is the next thing that needs to be loved.

The Seventh Practice

Love as much as you can from wherever you are.

The last practice is a major key because sometimes, in the heat of human relationships, you come to places in yourself or your partner that seem so hard to love that you feel the urge to give up. That is the moment when love and only love can heal. In those moments, you simply love yourself and your partner as much as you can from wherever you can, and the miracles come flowing back in.

SETH MEYERS, PSY.D., is a prominent author and psychologist in private practice in Los Angeles whose first book will be published in late 2010. Dr. Meyers has addressed relationship issues on *Good Morning America* and in such magazines as *Men's Health*, *Cosmopolitan*, *In Touch Weekly*, and *Women's Health & Fitness*, and he gives seminars on coping with relationship and other issues all over the United States. He writes his own blog on relationship issues as well as a popular blog for *Psychology Today*.

CREATING LOVE THAT LASTS

Seth Meyers, Psy.D.

Creating a happy marriage, everyone knows, requires mutual effort and perseverance. It's no easy feat to create a union strong enough to sustain you and your partner through the many cycles of life. As life throws you curveballs, injecting stressors and even possible personal tragedies into your respective life trajectories, you simply do your best to keep yourself and your relationship afloat.

In my work with couples, I have found that there is no neat or predetermined secret to romantic success — no recipe you can follow to bake the perfect marriage. Yet with enough thought and attention paid to your marriage, you can cultivate and sustain intimacy that lasts. Better still, you can create a relationship that will realize what I believe is a relationship's true purpose: to bring out the best in you and provide a nourishing platform from which you can catapult yourself forward and accomplish all the goals that you've dreamed of.

There's a perfectly good reason why so many books and poems have been written about love and marriage since paper and pen were first conceived: a successful relationship bears a certain mystique. Think about it; with how many individuals have you felt a true emotional and sexual connection in your life? You can probably capture that number on one or two hands. What draws one to another — particularly in a sexual sense — can be determined by no logarithm or theory of attraction. In fact, if you ask any man or woman inhabiting a happy, long-term marriage what drew each to the other initially, you'd discover what I find in my clinical practice: they're often hard-pressed to articulate the nature of the chemistry or why it works in the first place — they simply know it works.

From a psychological perspective, one of the most interesting facets of a happy relationship — and marriage marks no exception — is that it is rife with paradox. It's strange that something so beautiful, for many, often was born out of something so ugly: a past history of hurtful relationships with incompatible partners. You'll often find that some of the happiest marriages actually were preceded by a relationship that was fairly unhappy or, in some cases, downright awful. These scar-inducing past relationships often act as guides later to a better relationship. In other words, once hurt, you find a way to use the pain so that you avoid what didn't work in the past and point yourself towards a new, healthier type of partner in the future.

Regardless of what your past relationship history includes, you have the fundamental ability to create and sustain a happy marriage. I have isolated several factors that will help you to find and develop a marriage that works for you. In my practice with couples over the years, I have used these guiding principles as I show them a way to navigate the anxieties and fears inherent in loving someone so deeply. I am hopeful that you, too, can derive some meaning from these principles so that you accumulate your own romantic wisdom. Like the cold, winter ground that receives thick falling snowflakes in the midst of a snowstorm, I hope that you can breathe these principles in, adding layer upon layer to your preexisting understanding of yourself and your relationship. You can read about the first factor instrumental in creating a happy marriage below.

Balancing Attachment and Independence

Couples have all different kinds of relationship dynamics, and you can often see them on the surface when you socialize with them. I have always been struck in my clinical work to see how couples vary in terms of the degree to which they socialize separately as well as apart. I'm sure you know some couples who never socialize independently and only as a couple, while you can probably think of other couples where the opposite is true. Is there a correct level of independence to which couples should aspire? How much is too much time to spend together?

Typically, a therapist will tell you there is no right way of being, no identity template to which each individual should subscribe. For most therapists, it's all about subjectivity and shades of gray.

Yet, when it comes to the freedom partners allow each other in a relationship, I believe there is a bit of a right answer. While I acknowledge that there is a spectrum, I also acknowledge that women and men can too easily lose themselves (their interests, ambitions, and uniqueness) when they spend all their time with one person. In short, you can't fuse with another individual and expect to remain a separate and vibrant entity.

If your goal is to create and sustain a happy marriage, you must allow a fair amount of independence within the relationship. Couples who eat together, sleep together, go to their house of worship together, do everything socially together often take a turn down a dirt road that leads them straight to the romantic landfill. In my practice, I have found that couples who do everything together sometimes secretly feel claustrophobic in the relationship and wish they had more room to breathe and to be themselves. These pent-up feelings are dangerous because they often snowball, later morphing into deeper resentments.

When it comes to your own relationship, be sure to strike a balance between independence and attachment. If you love golf but your partner would rather chew glass than hit the golf course with you, go on your own and respect the differences between the two of you. Perhaps your partner will need a weekend away with friends at some point in the future, and you can use that opportunity to allow your partner to have some space. Ultimately, you should be checking in with your partner on an occasional basis about the quality of the relationship and update each other about day-to-day frustrations in the effort to otherwise avoid major meltdowns that follow months or years of repressed feelings. When you and your partner have a tête-à-tête and take inventory of the issues in your relationship, be sure to include the independence issue on your (figurative) relationship quality checklist.

Be Gentle with Each Other

Speaking of taking inventory of the overall quality of your relationship, another factor you'll want to consider relates to the way in which you and your partner relate to each other physically. Specifically, I'm talking about physical affection and the need for you to both give it and receive it in your relationship.

Before we continue, let me be clear that the physical affection I'm talking about is independent of sex or any touching that is intended to initiate sex. I am referring to the simplest physical gestures that are extended with gentleness and warmth, expressions of care and affection from one loved one to another. Such gestures could include rubbing a partner's back, giving a hug, or holding hands, among many others. Why, you might wonder, are such physical behaviors so important? In a nutshell, these gestures convey connection and kindness. More importantly, however, these behaviors are nonverbal expressions. While it is certainly heartwarming to hear your partner express warmth and love through words, the giving and receiving of affection through nonverbal means allows for an additional avenue of intimacy.

All too often, how expressive we are is a direct reflection of how demonstrative our families of origin were. If you come from a home in which there weren't regular displays of physical affection, you may not reach out to touch your partner on a regular basis. However, creating a happy marriage requires that you step out of your comfort zone, at times, and risk vulnerability for the sake of your own emotional growth and the intention to please your partner. To truly create and sustain a happy marriage, you'll need to constantly work to show your love in new ways, never surrendering entirely to routine expressions of love.

In your relationship, make an effort to express your love for your partner in a myriad of ways on a daily basis, and make physical affection a regular ingredient in your daily interactive dynamic. You can add warmth, intimacy, and spontaneity all in one shot by tenderly saying, "Give me your hand — let me give you a hand massage" as you watch your favorite television show together. The smallest gestures are often those that are most appreciated and best remembered. And ultimately, such overtures indicate an overall wish on your part to make your partner feel good. Going back to the basics — by means of giving physical affection — is a sure-fire way to keep you and your partner connected over the many years I hope the two of you will be together.

Keeping Passion Alive

While gentleness and physical affection are cornerstones of a healthy, long-term relationship, they will not provide sufficient sustenance to make a marriage work happily. Anyone married for many years will also tell you that keeping passion alive is equally important, and every marriage will navigate this challenge in different ways.

Before we dive too deeply into the issue, let me clarify the most important point: there are many different types of passion. Typically, we think of passion as sexual, but emotional and intellectual passion are equally important. In working with single clients who are looking for a relationship, I encourage them to find partners who share their interests and see the world in a similar way. By prioritizing these characteristics in their partner selection, they set the stage to find a truly compatible partner. In your own relationship, you can discover each other emotionally and intellectually for the rest of your lives — even when sexual urges have diminished.

Given this context, it won't surprise you that the first step to keeping passion alive is to accept that there are different kinds of passion. The next step is to learn to share a common interest or activity — something that allows the two of you to pass the time in a connected manner or to explore the world together. For some, this may include something as simple as playing cards, while for others, it may consist of something more complex, along the lines of having children and watching them grow, or following the news closely and having political discussions about current events. Overall, feeling emotionally and intellectually stimulated provides meaningful and lasting intimacy.

When it comes to sex and keeping passion alive, the third step is to remember to be open-minded and flexible. Understand that there are no rules — every couple is different. For some couples, sex is one of the main ways they communicate. For these couples, they may have sex frequently, from the very beginning of their relationship into the twilight years. For others, they may connect more in other ways, so they may turn to sex as a means of connecting less often.

The fourth and final step in keeping the passion alive is to openly discuss the sexual quality of your relationship to ensure that you are meeting each other's needs. A lull that goes on a little too long may signify feelings of sexual boredom, indicating that it's time to get out the relationship toolbox and repair the problem. If this scenario describes you or your relationship, ask your partner how he or she feels about your sex life, and share your feelings, too. Give your partner some ideas about things you'd like to try to bring some romance back, and ask your partner if he or she has any other ideas. By trial and error, try different things to see if any of them click. Remember that sex is a delicate topic, so approach the issue with your partner gently and fairly! Ultimately, be sure to discuss the issue — uncomfortable as it may be at first. You'll soon find that, when it comes to discussing awkward topics, actually practicing this behavior by broaching the subject makes it a little easier each time you try it.

Celebrating Your Anniversary
The last factor I will discuss in creating a happy marriage is simple:

obvious as it may seem, you must celebrate your anniversary. Many people frown on sentimentality, thinking that true sophisticates don't need silly rituals to prove or reinforce their love. Others simply get caught in the daily grind and allow certain social conventions to fall by the wayside. In your own relationship, you must remember to cherish your anniversary and to honor it with a formal occasion on an annual basis.

Celebrating an anniversary is a ritual, at root, and rituals provide a foundation for the way we organize ourselves in our lives. Specifically, conducting regular rituals helps to solidify your identity and remind you of what is most important to you. When it comes to the anniversary ritual, one of the reasons why it is so important is because it gives you a chance to remember how far you have come as a couple. It also gives you a chance to feel proud of yourself and of the two of you as a team.

We all know that relationships can be difficult and that they require effort, care, and attention. Moreover, a long-term marriage will bear the occasional hiccup, requiring that each partner navigate his or her feelings as they relate to the given issue. Such hiccups also introduce another challenge, and the couple must learn as a unit to communicate through that challenge. When you can transition through these challenges in your own relationship, you have grown as an individual and the two of you have grown as a couple.

As long as the marriage is still happy and each partner is getting his or her primary needs met, achieving another year together as a couple is a significant accomplishment. Always remember to celebrate your own anniversary in a special way so that you can truly breathe in the accomplishment that another year marks. After all, the anniversaries make some of the best memories!

A Few Final Thoughts

As I have previously said, the road to a happy and sustainable marriage is by no means smoothly paved or easily discovered — it's earned through consistent effort and attention paid to the quality of your relationship. Though hurdles will inevitably present themselves and nearly beckon you to run and hide, instead of directly confronting what's uncomfortable, take the challenge and face your emotional fears as you work to make your marriage a happy and lasting one.

In my clinical work, I often tell my clients that creating a loving marriage requires the greatest investment but yields the most significant rewards. Like an architect at your own drafting table, you have the ability to design the marriage you want from scratch and to renovate it as you see fit over the years. My hope for you is that you continually take inventory of your needs, as well as your partner's, from the very beginning, so that you build the kind of solid foundation that happily lasts a lifetime.

KRISTINE CARLSON is the coauthor with her husband, Richard Carlson, of such bestsellers as *Don't Sweat the Small Stuff in Love* and *Don't Sweat the Small Stuff for Women*. After Richard died unexpectedly at age forty-five of a pulmonary embolism, Kristine Carlson published a moving look at their marriage, the bestselling *An Hour to Live, An Hour to Love*, which contained a letter Richard had written in which he expressed his abiding love for her and pondered what would happen if he only had "an hour to live." She has spoken of love and loss in her appearances on *The Oprah Winfrey Show*, *The Today Show*, and *The View*. Her newest book is *Heartbroken Open: A Memoir Through Loss to Self-Discovery*.

THE SMALL THINGS WE DID THAT NOURISHED A LIFETIME OF LOVE

Kristine Carlson

A love relationship always starts out with attraction of one kind or another. Each of us has a "list" of qualities and characteristics that stands ready to be examined by our conscious mind, as well as "hidden lists" buried somewhere deep in our subconscious. These lists help us to define qualities that we might find appealing in a mate, from the physical to the ephemeral, the practical to the passionate.

When I met Richard Carlson, I was eighteen and had already developed a strong sense of my list and had even written down these aspects, clearly defining for myself what I might be looking for in a lifetime partner. However, I didn't expect to meet that man until much later in life.

The list included a number of youthful, superficial things: he had to be blonde, over six feet tall, good looking, and athletic. But, it also included the characteristics I found attractive in my father. He had to be gentle and kind, wise, loyal, passionate, intelligent, have a positive attitude and a discerning work ethic, and above all he had to have integrity and be honest to the bone.

Richard Carlson fulfilled this list and then some.

I believe part of why I recognized him immediately was because I had fully defined the characteristics and qualities of my perfect mate. One day, I noticed him walking with a friend just ahead of me — kicking up his heels and looking back. I knew the guy who was with him and yelled: "Hey, wait for me!" We sauntered back to our respective dorms on Seaver Drive at Pepperdine University, and an odd feeling settled in me.

I had an immediate feeling of familiarity and that I was somehow home. I also was just being myself without feeling like I had to impress him and that was a unique experience for me. We said goodbye, I walked upstairs to call my mother as I always did on Sundays, and she asked if I had met anyone interesting. Without thinking, and very innocently, I blurted: "Yes, I think I just met the man I'm going to marry." And, he hadn't even asked me out yet! Within one month we were inseparable and completely in love.

In the beginning it is the chemistry you feel that is the most powerful magnet, but it is the falling in love part of the equation that you want to sustain — that indescribable good feeling, which nourishes that initial connection like water and sunshine to a sunflower. It's easy in the beginning because we fall into each other in euphoria, but how do we sustain that love as it stands the test of time? How do we create a marriage that we love for a lifetime?

The other day I asked my oldest daughter, Jasmine, what she had seen about Richard's and my relationship that made it different than others. She replied: "You and dad were great friends who didn't argue and pick at each other the way other couples do. You were best friends and treated each other that way." It's true that Richard and I talked about the most important aspects of a great relationship and wrote a hundred chapters on how to keep that loving connection alive in *Don't Sweat the Small Stuff in Love.* We determined that being pals first, respecting one another, listening to each other, and sharing the same core values were among the most important aspects to creating a partnership you love. It was also equally important to laugh a lot and keep the relationship playful and fun, because so much of life gets to be all too serious, especially after you have children.

We had an early morning ritual of waking before dawn, making our coffee, meditating, and then spending a couple of hours talking and listening and strategizing about how to live better and just be present with one another. As we opened our eyes at the end of meditation, we would pause to share a moment in each other's gaze. This was our time and even when Richard traveled or I was away we called each other every morning with a cup of coffee in hand.

Early on in our marriage, Richard and I were like two stones tumbling and polishing one another. We designed a practice, which taught us how to speak to each other lovingly while hearing each other without becoming defensive. Instead of allowing small issues to fester and turn into something big, each of us had the desire to clarify or make the small changes necessary to foster our love connection, and we knew that heartfelt communication and listening would be necessary to a loving marriage. We devised a weekly weekend ritual in which we would sit facing each other cross-legged on the floor. We would take turns speaking to one another and the speaker would hold a crystal heart. The listener would stay present and would remain quiet until the speaker was finished. After that, the listener would reflect what was heard by saying: "I hear what you are saying is…" In this practice we would often find that what was said and what was heard were two completely different things.

We would pass the heart back and forth, taking turns listening and speaking, repeating this process until we usually ended our session rolling with laughter because much of the small stuff that bothered us during the week became funny after speaking it out loud.

What we also discovered was that we were like mirrors, reflecting each other's feelings back to ourselves. For example, if I was feeling taken for granted in some way, Richard also felt that way. We often balanced these talks by closing our time together naming the things we noticed about each other or the acts of kindness from that week that we were grateful for. The beauty of this technique was that long after we stopped practicing it formally, we had created a foundation for how we communicated about daily issues. And, believe me, over the course of our twenty-five years together, we had our fair share of issues to work out and to discuss in our relationship with each other and our daughters. So having a dependable structure of healthy communication habits stemming from our rituals was a blessing. We learned how to relate to each other with respect and honor, staying highly tuned in to each other in a practice of listening.

Marriage is a union like no other, which requires each person to love themselves wholly and completely while giving 100 percent of that love back through the doorway of commitment to the relationship. In a healthy marriage there is a balance between the "I" as in the individual and the "we" of the partnership together. There are questions we asked ourselves every day, such as: How can I make my spouse's life easier or better today while being true to myself? How can I create peace and harmony within myself so that I may bring that to my love relationship? How can I align with my partner's perspective and also agree that sometimes we are just going to disagree? How can I not take my partner's low moods personally? Asking and answering these questions as a practice kept us on track throughout the years. The cornerstone of our healthy relationship became taking personal responsibility for our individual happiness while doing the small things that took care of each other, often placing the needs of one another before the needs of the self. This was a beautiful waltz and an egoless path of love as we danced through life together.

In our marriage we came together to build a temple and it was stronger because the two of us participated fully. We also allowed space for each of us to move through this temple as separate beings with individual expression.

Later, as our family grew and we raised Jazz and Kenna, it became my role to hold Richard's space with the family while he did his spiritual work through his writing. Our trust in each other and open communication helped him move about freely in the world while doing his work because he never had to worry about the foundation of his family.

One of the small ways I knew I could make Richard's life easier was to release him from family responsibilities for days at a time so he could write unencumbered. He used to call me and thank me with such heartfelt appreciation that I would give him that time. I knew he needed space and stillness to tap into his inspiration fully and also to enjoy the process. And unlike most men in our culture, he made it easy to give him the space he needed because he was so present on a regular basis with our family and practical life. In our home, there weren't gender models for who did the cooking and cleaning. We both shared all responsibilities and did what needed to be done in the moment. We tossed a ball back and forth; catch and release.

We didn't experience "ownership" in our marriage, in the way that can sometimes happen when a partner becomes like an armchair, cozy and protective, that, over time, loses its novelty due to familiarity. We made it a practice to express our appreciation daily for all the small, invisible ways each of us contributed to our household. Richard often left notes of love and appreciation for me so that I would find them while he was away. I would make it a point to thank him for being such an amazing husband, father, and provider for our family — and I really meant it when I looked into his eyes and spoke the truth to him.

The true reverence we shared for one another fed our devotion to our partnership and our family. We nurtured what started out as a seed and grew into an abundant harvest of fruitful gifts. We put our love relationship first, knowing the greatest gift we could give our children was peace and harmony in our marriage. We felt abiding love, but we also really liked each other, too. We just enjoyed hanging out together and it didn't matter what we did. We could sit in complete silence and do nothing at all. We laughed a lot at ourselves and the absurdity of life, and we always played together like children.

We knew our way of relationship was rare, but I never fully appreciated all that we shared until his unexpected death from a pulmonary embolism in December 2006. Before that, I had taken for granted that life would remain the same and there would be many more years ahead.

I always said that a lifetime of loving Richard would not be enough. Now I can clearly see all the nuances of our relationship that were once invisible because we were so involved in living. Now I more clearly understand how the infinite capacity of commitment to love can be the structure and foundation of a great relationship and truly intimate experience. Our marriage was solid and happy; it stood the test of time, and now it reveals itself to be a continuously nourishing bond. It is evident to me now that it was the small things we did for each other every day that sustained our connection for a lifetime. While Richard is no longer in form, I feel his presence in my heart often guiding and comforting me as I carry on. It is the love connection that we nourished in life together through the portal of marriage that has strengthened me to continue to live life fully and to live for the both of us now.

As you enter my home, there is a photo of Richard in the center of an E.E. Cummings quote that reads:

> *i carry your heart with me*
> *(i carry it in my heart)*
> *i am never without it*
> *(anywhere i go you go, my dear...)*

Treasure the gifts of life and love.

NICOLE CHAISON chronicles "the roller coaster of passion that is parenting" in her celebrated self-published quarterly, *Hausfrau Mutha-zine*, which has generated a loyal cult following. She is the author of the graphic work of nonfiction, *The Passion of the Hausfrau*, which *Publishers Weekly* hailed as "innovative," as well as the one-woman play based on the book. She wrote the James Beard award – nominated *Spice: Flavors of the Eastern Mediterranean* with Chef Ana Sortun, and her stories and comics have appeared in *MotherWords*, *Fertile Ground*, and the collection *Forty Things To Do When You Turn Forty*, published by Sellers Publishing.

the MARRIAGE TRIP

NICOLE CHAISON

AND SO I'm THINKING...

... AND BLAH BLAH BLAH..

SHE/HE

I WISH HE'D PUT HIS ARMS AROUND ME + SNUGGLE.

I WISH SHE'D STOP TALKING + HAVE SEX WITH ME.

YIN/YANG

YOGA IS A PRACTICE. AND ONLY THROUGH PRACTICE IS THERE PROGRESS. YOU CAN PRACTICE ANYTHING...

ALICE

was lying

in bed with my hubby, Craig, telling him about this assignment I'm working on for a collection called "Creating a Marriage You'll Love" and trying to get him to brainstorm with me about the subject (the building blocks that create a good marriage, for example). But as usual, I was hogging the airtime with my stream-of-conscious rambling, and my hubby was just wishing I'd shut up and take off my clothes and jump his bones. That wasn't about to happen—not with my mind all awhirl on a subject like that, and so I kept talking until I noticed Craig was snoring.

Cut to the next day: I'm off to yoga class, and of course my teacher Alice says something while we were doing half-pigeon that totally transported me to another plane (not this one that I was in right there: in which my right leg was bent at a 90 degree angle inward and my torso lay flat against it, so that my right hip flexors were stretched to capacity). Half-pigeon has a way of making me weepy and vulnerable-feeling, especially if I'm struggling with something in my personal life outside the yoga studio.

But what was I struggling with?

Alice instructed us to be present to the sensations, and if we were feeling discomfort, or like we wanted to get out of the pose, then that means the pose is just starting. I really wanted to get out of that pose.

So I breathed and felt some tears and beads of sweat roll down my forehead and nose and plop onto my yoga mat. My right hip yelled at me to get out of half-pigeon pose—or else. My mind skittered around inside my skull, like a squirrel caught in a Have-a-Heart trap, looking for an out—any out.

I was finally able to escape the present moment's discomfort by cogitating on my assignment for "Creating a Marriage You'll Love." What would I write about?

How about the discipline of marriage? The daily *practice* of marriage. As Alice said, *you can practice anything.* Does creating a marriage you love have to do with *practicing,* just like you'd practice any discipline for which you have a passion?

But then Alice started talking about a practice's inevitable plateaus.

And what is a plateau, in marital terms? Feeling disconnected from your partner. Out of synch. Not close. Like something's awry but it's hard to name. Hard to talk about.

In a plateau, I take my partner for granted. I coast along in daily habits without being mindful of his humanity. I lose perspective and become irritable and focus on the unpleasant small stuff (the way he loads the dishwasher with the bowls all jammed together so they don't get clean inside; the way he drops his towel on the floor after

he showers and forgets to hang it up, no matter how many times I pleasantly remind him). I forget to appreciate the magic in the everyday, in him. I maybe even lose sight of loving him.

Alice eventually released us from half-pigeon, and I stretched my legs in downward-facing dog. God, it felt good. And I now had a jumping-off point for my story.

But I felt uncomfortable about making pronouncements on the daily practice of *my* marriage—and its plateaus—because I was starting to suspect that Craig and I were in one such plateau at that moment, and perhaps we had been in the plateau for so long that we had lost sight of other possibilities.

Plus, I'll be honest here: the tenacity with which I attempted to escape the discomfort of half-pigeon is an indication of how I deal with discomfort in pretty much every area of my life. Part of practice is sitting with (and eventually working through) discomfort. So after yoga class, I turned to gurus far and wide for answers.

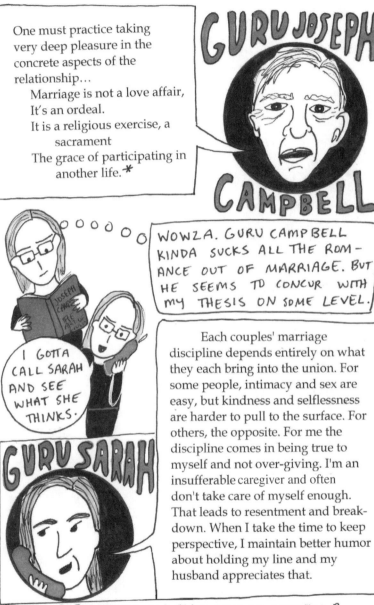

One must practice taking very deep pleasure in the concrete aspects of the relationship...
Marriage is not a love affair, It's an ordeal.
It is a religious exercise, a sacrament
The grace of participating in another life. *

GURU JOSEPH CAMPBELL

WOWZA. GURU CAMPBELL KINDA SUCKS ALL THE ROMANCE OUT OF MARRIAGE. BUT HE SEEMS TO CONCUR WITH MY THESIS ON SOME LEVEL.

I GOTTA CALL SARAH AND SEE WHAT SHE THINKS.

GURU SARAH

Each couples' marriage discipline depends entirely on what they each bring into the union. For some people, intimacy and sex are easy, but kindness and selflessness are harder to pull to the surface. For others, the opposite. For me the discipline comes in being true to myself and not over-giving. I'm an insufferable caregiver and often don't take care of myself enough. That leads to resentment and break-down. When I take the time to keep perspective, I maintain better humor about holding my line and my husband appreciates that.

* FROM REFLECTIONS ON THE ART OF LIVING : A JOSEPH CAMPBELL COMPANION (HARPERCOLLINS, 1991). PAGES 46-47.

SO THEN I TEXTED MY FRIEND TOM TO SEE WHAT HE PRACTICED IN HIS MARRIAGE DISCIPLINE...

My marriage practice is about submission to this fact: You cannot, neither by means of sheer will nor practical engagement, force your spouse to change. One's energy is much better spent on changing the self.

Also, make your spouse's world a better place. She will be happier in it.

And, no adult really wants to be one. Purposely maintain a level of childish wonder that you and your spouse can share.

And, no guns in the house.

And, keep as few secrets from your spouse as possible. Honesty should be the default approach.

And, lots of oral sex. And I mean lots.

GURU TOM

HAVE YOU AND CINDY EVER HIT A MARITAL PLATEAU ???

The thing about plateaus is you don't know you're on one until you've been there for a while and by then you're kind of used to walking on flat ground. It's nice, so much easier than the climb up.

My marriage has survived many a plateau, marked most notably by withdrawal on both our parts. Communication dropped off and along with it went intimacy. Withholding one's sadness from those who love you the most only deepens the gloom. That's a dangerous path to find oneself on. What do you call a wife or husband who won't talk to you? A roommate.

My practice is about accepting that my life and my marriage are like a deeply messy junk drawer. It's inexplicable and has some moldy unrecognizable stuff in the corners, but it seems to have everything I need in it, and best of all, it's full of surprises.

I LATER EMAILED MY FRIEND, CHRISTINE, BECAUSE I KNEW SHE WOULD HAVE SOME JUICY MUSINGS TO SHARE.

toppity tap tap

mmm... I LIKE THAT.

tap tap

tappity tap

GURU CHRISTINE

HOW DO YOU GET THROUGH THE MARITAL PLATEAUS?

You need to find moments of enchantment in the mind-numbing minutia of living daily with another person.

CAN YOU GIVE ME AN EXAMPLE OF THE ENCHANTMENT YOU MENTIONED?

tappity tap

8:00 a.m., Saturday, I'm on a soggy soccer field, the most miserable place on earth. We are not sports people, or morning people, but my daughter has joined a soccer team with all her six-year old pals, and she LOVES it. I'm huddled over my extra-large coffee throwing stink-eye at anyone who dares come near me, thinking about the bad karma I must have to land me *HERE this early on a weekend.*

My husband lopes up, and somehow gets roped into being a line referee for the game. What ensues is like a cross between Buster Keaton, Dick Van Dyke, and Fred McMurray as the Absent Minded Professor. My husband doesn't know the rules of the game, how to call a ball in or out, and keeps waving the flag the wrong way.

(CHRISTINE'S STORY IS CONTINUED ON NEXT PAGE)

Occasionally he trips, and the other refs blow their whistles, thinking he is waving his flag at them when really he's just trying to regain his balance. Helpful little girls keep handing him the ball back because he's constantly giving it to the wrong team for throw-ins. Then, just when he seems to be getting the hang of it, it's half-time and the teams switch sides, like they're playing a prank specifically on him.

I can see how some wives might be embarrassed by their husband's total incompetence displayed publically, or how they might even get angry, if they cared about the actual outcome of the game, but I laugh until I practically fall out of my lawn chair. And then I notice how beautiful the early morning light is, and how pleasant it is to have hot coffee steam blowing in my face, and how cute my kid looks in her *Bend It Like Beckham* clothes, and I'm so happy to be there, with HIM: the man tripping over his own shoelaces.

SO SWEET! I LIKE THIS IDEA OF ACTIVELY SEEKING JOY AND ENCHANTMENT IN DAY-TO-DAY LIVING WITH YOUR SPOUSE.

SHARON! IS JOY PART OF YOUR MARRIAGE PRACTICE?

ABSOLUTELY!

GURU SHARON

Every chance we get, as small as it may be, we find the things to make us joyful. We make a point of stopping to look at sleeping babies (our own and other peoples'), a full bright moon, a butterfly. We dance every chance we get. Usually like complete goofballs, so that we make each other & ourselves laugh while we are at it. When we see something funny on a TV show, we will grab the remote and just keep playing it over and over again to see how hard it can make us laugh for how long.

LATER ON, I TOOK A BREAK + HAD A CUP OF TEA WITH MY NEIGHBOR, ANNA. I JUST HAD TO ASK HER ABOUT WHAT SHE DOES IN MARITAL PLATEAUS.

GURU ANNA

I'd call my strategy "poke at things until something shifts." I'm pretty sure it's not the most pleasant strategy to live with. But I gotta tell you, sometimes it works. Or maybe it just seems to work because we're going to get off the plateau sooner or later anyway, and if I poke and prod enough it will coincide with that hop off the plateau.

Some of my less-than-admirable poking strategies: I poured water on my husband once when he didn't want to talk to me but was just going to go to bed. I've piled up his stuff on his side of the bed so that he could have a visual representation of all the crap he leaves around for me to pick up.

I'm not trying to say my poking is good. It's not bad, either. It's just what I do when I am frustrated that we've been unconnected for too long and I miss my husband. What is unconnected anyway? It's a feeling that we're not on the same page, that we don't know what the other is up to, that we aren't actively supporting one another or creating mutual things together.

What I have going for me is that I love my husband and I married him. I picked him. Nobody forced me into this marriage. I chose him for everything he is and is not. So even when we're stuck on a plateau, I have faith in him, in me, and in our relationship. I get impatient and want off the plateau and a return to feeling connected, yes. And underneath that impatience is a strong faith in what we can create with one another. I know that we're eventually coming back to each other and I just want it to be sooner rather than later.

THE NEXT EVENING, I WENT OUT TO DINNER WITH MY GIRLFRIENDS. THE TOPIC OF CONVERSATION? YOU GUESSED IT!

My hubby and I are always practicing better communication. We get books about improving relationships out from the library and read them in bed together. This works just as good as therapy, sometimes better, because the authors are experts in their fields. The money we save from therapy can go towards a night out on the town.

It sounds super cheesy—and maybe I just had too many sports coaches at an impressionable age)—but I really think that the best times in our marriage are when we're working together. When we need to refocus, it helps for us to have a project, which is probably why the homesteading life is so appealing to us. If we've been feeling out of sync with each other, sometimes getting back on track is a simple as "You hold the goat, I'll trim the hooves," or in the case of this weekend, "You kill the poultry and I'll eviscerate it."

Thank-yous go an enormous way in our relationship. Sometimes after a hectic morning of getting everyone fed, washed, dressed, and delivered, I'll call Steve on my way to work and thank him for one small kindness he added to our morning, like emptying the dishwasher, or making a cranky child laugh.

GURU MARGI GURUS WILLA + SHARON

WHEN I GOT HOME, I HAD AN EMAIL FROM MY FRIEND STEVE — RESPONDING TO A QUESTION I'D ASKED HIM ABOUT MARRIAGE EARLIER THAT WEEK.

I'D WONDERED ABOUT WHAT HIS MARITAL PLATEAUS WERE + HOW HE + HIS WIFE DEALT WITH THEM.

tap

tappity tap

GURU STEVE

tap tap

I don't agree with this plateau notion. Our marriage is a roller coaster, not a series of interrupted plateaus. The lows, which often are crisis-like, are often preceded by a faux plateau–a time of apparent equanimity that usually hides some slowly worsening flaw that finally brings us down into some horrible fight about something. We fight with great intensity. Lightning bolts snap out of the floors and ceilings, leaving us exhausted, sometimes numb, but as the skies clear we regain ourselves and our love, refreshed.

I LOVED THE CANDOR OF GURU STEVE'S ANSWER... AND IT RANG TRUE FOR ME AND CRAIG AS WELL. WOULD WE FIGHT TO MOVE OFF THIS PLATEAU? AND THEN I GOT A MESSAGE FROM MY FRIEND BETH.

tappity tap tap

tappity tap tap

GURU BETH

To move through a plateau, you've got to have humor, an ability to come together. Having sex is key, too. It's a great way to reconnect (no pun intended) besides all the other obvious pleasures.

JOSEPH BAILEY is a noted marriage and family counselor, author, university teacher, and consultant to major businesses. Bailey won international recognition for pioneering important concepts regarding the prevention of addiction. He is the coauthor with Richard Carlson of the bestselling *Slowing Down to the Speed of Life*, which has been translated into twenty-six languages worldwide, and the author of such highly acclaimed books as *The Serenity Principle*, *The Speed Trap*, *Slowing Down to the Speed of Love*, and *Fearproof Your Life*.

T R U E   L O V E

Joseph   Bailey

Falling in Love

Perhaps the closest many of us come to experiencing true love is when we first fall in love with another human being. I remember when I first fell in love with my wife, Michael, almost thirty years ago. We were both attending a seminar in Miami at the invitation of our mutual best friends, who were, coincidently, married to each other. Part of their ulterior motive in inviting us to the seminar was to have us meet. Even before I met Michael, I knew she was special. As my friends told me about her on the phone, something began to stir within me. They spoke of her free, artistic spirit, her spiritual depth, and her fearless spontaneous nature. They also said she was fun to be with and very attractive. I felt my heart opening up and I experienced a very strong curiosity and "pull" to meet her. I couldn't stop wondering about her as the time approached to fly to Miami for the seminar.

I'll never forget picking Michael up from the Miami International Airport. I was struck by her beauty, but even more by her presence.

I felt attracted to her, but not in the same way that I had been attracted to other women. There was something qualitatively different that I couldn't understand. I felt as though we had always known each other and that we were simply reconnecting after a long absence.

As I got to know her on that long weekend, I fell deeply in love. It was magical! When we walked along the streets of Coral Gables, we held hands and kissed by each palm tree. I experienced an energy from holding hands that felt so warm and comforting and ran all the way to the center of my heart. I had never felt anything like this before. I wanted to know everything about her, but mostly I just loved the feeling I was experiencing being with her. When I was with Michael, I felt a joyful aliveness and a freedom to just be myself. Her free spirit allowed others around her to be whoever they were with no judgment. Michael was very focused on her own spiritual realization and was unwavering in her pursuit of the Truth. It felt so natural to be together that I knew I had met my soul mate. People at the seminar were surprised when we said that we had just met that weekend. Many commented that they thought we had been together a long time. We had found true love.

During our five days together, I experienced a new reality. I felt like I did as young boy — joyful, everything seeming more vivid and colorful, my senses awake in a way they hadn't been in decades. No wonder people love to fall in love, I thought. It was a stark contrast to the serious young man I had become after my divorce and years of graduate education in psychology, where I had learned to constantly analyze myself and everyone else. I was living in my intellect detached from my true spirit of well-being, while (ironically) I was trying to help others find happiness and satisfaction in their relationships and families as their counselor. Before that weekend, I was feeling burned out, stressed by my life, and discouraged by what I had hoped to find in life.

That weekend at the seminar I also discovered some principles about mental health that would profoundly change not only my personal life but my professional work as well. A new paradigm of psychology, based on bringing out the innate health and resiliency of clients rather than "fixing" their issues and diseases, was presented at the seminar. These ideas shook my professional world as a therapist and teacher. They pointed me toward a sense of my own well-being and showed me how to help my clients understand the principles of how the mind works.

I wondered at the time, what was this exhilarating feeling I was experiencing. Was it true love or was it like so many infatuations I had experienced in the previous twenty years that had ended in disappointment and the fear that true love was just an illusion? Or was it that the new insights I had that weekend about the nature of mental health had changed my whole life? Perhaps both were true.

A Personal and Professional Paradigm Shift

What I now realize is that what I experienced that weekend in Miami was a whole life transformation and true love. I not only found my true love, I found my True Self. Falling in love helped me begin to understand how life worked on a profound level, that true love was my birthright and that I had it within me all along. Falling in love temporarily broke the trance of my habitual way of seeing life and I was able to see the truth of who Michael was, who I was, and what life was. The result of cracking through my ego was experienced as love — because love is who we are at our deepest core. When we fall in love, the veil of judgment, fear, and illusion falls away, and with it we fall — *into* love. Most of my life, except for a few early years, I had spent in the prison of my self-created thought system, filled with insecurity and a profound longing for something that I couldn't find and didn't even know how to begin searching for.

The Nature of True Love

True love — we hear this phrase often, but what is its real meaning? True love is a state of consciousness that is able to transcend the habitual ways of seeing life. When we fall in love, we see the true essence of the object of our love — the truth of the other person.

True love is innate to our being; it is in our hearts, waiting for us to discover it as our true nature. This is why most of us so longingly search for love. Like our hearts that are perpetually beating, love is ever-present. However, we seldom become aware of it unless we fall in love, have a transcendent experience or a moment of extreme presence when we are able to see the beauty of nature, art, music, or are deeply touched by the love of another person. In these experiences we discover what has always been dormant within us — true love.

Some say true love is rare, fleeting, can't be found, or that it can't last. If true love is always within our hearts, then why does it seem so desperately out of our reach, or so easily lost, or taken for granted when the concerns and worries of our troubled lives seem to sweep over love and submerge it with negativity, stress, and distraction?

That is the question this essay on true love will address — what true love is and how to keep it alive in our relationship and ourselves, allowing that feeling of love to permeate our whole lives.

The True Self

What I experienced that weekend in Miami and for much of the past thirty years, was not new, but more of a remembering of something I knew when I came into the world — a primordial memory of my true identity, my True Self. Falling in love, finding true love, is a glimpse back to our original True Self.

As young children most of us experience this natural Self, before we begin to develop our ego self — the sum total of our personal habitual thoughts that we begin to identify with and call "me." The ego is comprised of all the labels, beliefs, and ideas we call the personality. The natural Self is the feeling of unconditional joy and contentment, curiosity about life, living fully in the present moment free of worry, and of being in awe of the simplicity of life. As we move away from the awareness of our True Self, we begin to feel fearful and alone. As we become disconnected from who we truly are, we develop a complex set of thoughts, beliefs, and concepts about everything from who we are, to the nature of relationships, life, and everything else. This thought system becomes a filter through which we view and create our reality. By identifying with our thoughts about life and ourselves, we create a false sense of self — the ego.

The ego is an illusionary self, separated from the true essence of our being, and is the cause of all of our suffering, unhappiness, and insecurities. When we live separate from our true nature, we live in a false or illusionary reality where none of our true needs and desires can be fulfilled. Living from ego is also what causes us to doubt true love, to fall out of love, or to destroy love when we find it. It stops us from listening to our wisdom, our insights, our dreams, and our purpose in life. Most of all, it causes us to lose hope for what we could be if we were to experience the fullness of life.

Love Is Letting Go of Fear

When I returned to Minnesota from Miami, I couldn't stop thinking about Michael. The feelings of new love didn't stop growing in the absence of our being together. On the contrary, these feelings began to deepen and my whole experience of life began to change. That is, until fear returned to my mind.

"What if she doesn't feel the same way I do?" "What if this experience of falling in love is like all the others — fleeting, temporary, disappointing in the end, and heartbreaking?" These thoughts and many others led me to doubt my earlier strong feelings for Michael so much that I didn't call her for two weeks. I was caught up in my ego again and full of fear.

But the feelings of love kept growing in spite of my fear, and I finally began to listen to my heart and called her. I told her that my feelings of love were growing each day. To my relief, she felt the same way.

We talked on the phone every night and the feelings of love grew even deeper. Two months later I visited her for five days and at the end of that time we both realized that one of us would have to move because we could no longer bear to be apart. After two more months Michael moved to Minnesota, as I had a young son from my first marriage and a private practice. She had nothing holding her in Texas, so she came to join me on this journey. A year later we married, but in reality we had felt married almost from the moment we met. We each had found true love.

If I had listened to my fears, I would not have let love in and we would never have experienced the love in our hearts. But this tale of love doesn't end here.

The Temptation of Fear

I remember the first trial in our relationship. Many months of blissful love passed before I had my first fearful thought attack. I was lying in the bathtub, obsessing about the fact that Michael didn't have any health insurance and didn't seem the least concerned about it. She was an artist and a free spirit and never even considered the necessity of having a health insurance policy in place. In my family, having insurance was as important as a college education, a good job, and settling down and raising a family. She didn't have the same fine print in her script for a happy life and I feared this wasn't the only difference we had. As I lay there in the tub, I became more concerned, confused, and threatened by this first collision of our values and beliefs.

I shouted to the bedroom from the tub, "Michael, we have to talk."

"What is it, Joe?" she said nervously, probably thinking that my serious tone of voice could mean only one thing: a break up.

"Insurance!" I announced, as if it should be obvious what was on my mind.

"Insurance?" she called back incredulously.

"Yes, insurance! I can't believe you don't have health insurance and don't seem to care."

She started to laugh, thinking I must be joking. It was understandable for her to think I was kidding, since she had not yet seen that serious side of me, as I had been lighthearted and in love the whole time thus far in our relationship.

"Insurance is what this is all about? Joe, you've got to be kidding me."

Sensing her disbelief I suddenly felt foolish. I hesitated, but then my ego defensively kicked in and I went into a tirade about the value and importance of insurance and said that if we were going to be a couple she would need it.

Relieved we weren't breaking up and yet perplexed by our

discussion, Michael agreed to get insurance but she was shocked to see this other side of me.

At that moment I had unconsciously chosen fear rather than love and it created our first mini-crisis — one of many that have occurred whenever I have fallen out of my True Self and into my ego thoughts with all their fears, insecurities, and expectations. Luckily for us, Michael and I have gradually gained an understanding of how to create our experience in order to sustain the feelings of true love and immunize ourselves from the habits of our egos. So, how do we sustain the feeling of being in love? What are the principles that have allowed both of us to fall deeper in love in spite of our many habits of fearful thinking that can obscure our true feelings for one another?

Sustaining Love

If falling out of love seems to happen so frequently in our marriages, then once we have been fortunate to find true love, how do we sustain it? Or, if our love has begun to fade, or is barely flickering, how do we bring it back to life? In other words, how do we keep love alive in a world that seems so inhospitable to love, a world that seems to thrive on stress, conflict, and negativity? This section will focus on the guidelines for sustaining true love in marriage.

If we have a beautiful plant in our home that is in full flower when we buy it from the florist, how do we keep it blooming, healthy, green, and lush? Obviously we must not take it for granted or it will soon dry up, lose its blooms and leaves, and eventually die. The same is true with love.

The neglect of love in a marriage takes the form of getting caught up in the busyness of our daily lives — our work demands, the challenges of parenting, and the infinite distractions of cell phones, email, texting, TV, and the onslaught of information that comes to us each day. In the flurry of such a busy life, that small plant of love often gets ignored.

To sustain love we must choose to place a part of our awareness, time, and energy toward the growing and nurturing of our true love. In the case of a plant, it requires sunlight, water, fertilizer, pruning, and occasionally transplanting. In our marriage, it takes the following ingredients to keep love alive and constantly growing and transforming:

Deep listening

Presence

Choice

Seeing the True Self in ourselves and our partner

Forgiveness

Deep Listening

In my seminars, counseling, and retreats, I often tell couples and individuals that if I could pass on only one thing to help them sustain their lives and relationships, it would be to help them discover the art of deep listening. Deep listening is listening beyond the words of another person to the heart or essence of what it is they are attempting to say or point to. Deep listening requires that the person listening is not in his or her head (analyzing, judging, labeling, rehearsing, or being distracted by irrelevant thoughts), but instead is listening with his or her heart for the grain of truth that is implicit. It is a kind of listening rare in our modern world — one that requires a state of deep presence of mind.

When a person listens deeply, the other person is far more interesting to the listener. This practice calms one down and creates a strong feeling of connectedness to the other person. The person being listened to feels respected, understood, and cared for in the most intimate way. When I listen deeply to Michael, I feel I am allowing her the space and love to heal, forgive, and have insights about her situation. Listening deeply creates a heart-to-heart connection where each is once again able to see the True Self of the other person. The results are feelings of compassion, kindness, patience, and a restoration and sustainability of true love.

To practice deep listening, you need only to be willing to catch yourself in the act of not listening when you become distracted, judgmental, impatient to speak and interrupt, preoccupied with your own thoughts, or involved in trying too hard to listen. Deep listening is a state of focused yet relaxed awareness. Be aware of when you are not listening and then, without judging yourself, gently bring yourself back to the present and to the sincere intention of listening. This will bring you back to deep listening. Over time you will get better and better at this skill, and you and your partner will build confidence in each other to communicate in ways you've never even dreamed of.

Presence

Related to deep listening is the practice of being present, which simply means living in the present moment. So many of us rarely live in the "now" of our lives; instead, we rush from one future moment to another, missing the precious moment that is always in front of us. We are so caught up in striving for success, the perfect home and other possessions, planning for some future time when we can relax, that we miss the only time that actually exists — the here and now.

Sometimes couples will tell me that it is in situations when they are jolted into the moment — during a crisis, during a winter storm when the electricity has gone off — that they are forced by circumstances to actually be present. In the present moment, we are able to calm down and see the beauty that surrounds us or is in our loved ones, and we feel grateful. In the present moment, we discover that we are enough, we have enough, and life is a blessing. Choosing to be present is another secret to intimacy and sustaining true love. We don't have to wait for a crisis to force us into presence — it is always available once we are aware of our thinking and emotions.

Living in the moment doesn't preclude planning for the future or remembering the past and what we have learned. But it is in a state of presence that we are able to intuit the proper amount of time spent planning and reflecting and remembering the past so that it doesn't get in the way of living in the moment, where life really exists. Living in the moment is practical and allows us to creatively respond to life as it comes.

The Power of Choice

Mind is the Universal Intelligence that we are all a part of, not to be confused with the useful, but limited intellect. It is the most powerful force in our lives. From this life force comes the power to think, to perceive, to feel, to act, and to create our lives. Realizing that we are the creator of our moment-to-moment experience of life gives us the responsibility and the freedom to create the quality of life and relationships we desire. Most of us create our lives unconsciously from the habits of our past conditioning, memories, beliefs, and prejudices, without ever knowing we are doing it. We can also create our lives from the True Self that is at one with the Universal Intelligence.

To live in love, we must choose to live in our True Self and to reject the habits of the ego. How do we know what we are choosing? By being in touch with our feelings. We are either coming from love or from fear. Just listen to yourself and be honest and see if the feeling that is directing your decisions, actions, and motives is based in love or fear. If you choose the path of love, you will sustain true love. If you choose fear, you will create suffering, distance, mistrust, anger, and a host of other negative emotions.

I recently heard about a couple that had been in an intensive therapy program with a colleague of mine. At the end of the program, they had made a significant breakthrough after years of bitterness, suffering, and a near divorce. They left the last session in a state of bliss. The therapist warned them that the transformation process to become their True Selves involved a great deal of slipping back into their ego habits and to not be discouraged if they returned to old familiar feelings of hopelessness, anger, and frustration. What was important was their commitment to be willing to be true to themselves and to forgive each other and themselves, again and again, as they moved towards their goal of transformation.

Sure enough, their bliss at the end of the last session was short-lived and they called the next day saying that the good feelings had all blown up. The therapist remained calm and understanding about what was happening. He reminded them of his warning and the importance of remaining committed, open, and willing to forgive. He could see how far they had come, but they felt like they were back at square one. His perspective helped them regain their bearings and with it the hope and forgiveness they needed to return to the true love that was there the day before.

The process of transformation to true love and our True Self is a spiral rather than a straight line. What appears to be a failure or regression to our old selves is really an opportunity to experience our old ego habit with more awareness and more of a sense of choice. Each time we choose our True Self, we are rewarded with more insights and more confidence in our ability to find our resilience.

JOSEPH BAILEY

Seeing Health, Love, and the True Self
in Our Partner and Ourselves

It is so easy to find fault in our mate. We see them at their best and their worst. Unfortunately, when we are guided by our ego, we feel self-protective and tend to focus on and anticipate only their worst aspect — their habitual ego self. Soon we will see them only as that, and not as the True Self that we fell in love with.

Over years of marriage, it is easy to store all the hurts, disappointments, breaches of trust, and shortcomings, and forget who our loved one really is. Choosing to see beyond our habits and those of our mate will restore hope and confidence so that we live life based on who we really are. Forgiveness, which we will talk about in the next section, is the healing balm that clears our perception based on past memories. It allows us to once again see the truth of our partner and our self.

Whenever Michael is able to keep her True Self perspective when I am in an old habit of my ego, she is patient, honest, and non-reactive. By responding to my ego with love, and by staying grounded in her True Self, Michael helps me recognize my ego more quickly than if we get into a familiar tango dance of habit together. Recently, I was feeling insecure about a long trip she was about to take with her sister. We had never been apart for such a long time and I was making up all kinds of negative thoughts in my head about her trip. I asked for a heart-to-heart talk and divulged my insecurities to her. Rather than get angry or defensive, she simply listened deeply and lovingly and then reiterated her deep love for me and helped me to realize that the trip said nothing about us as a couple. She didn't do her half of the tango and so I was left alone on the dance floor of dysfunction. I calmed down very quickly and soon realized that I had jumped back into my ego habits of the past. I felt grateful to her for not reacting to my regression when I had reverted back to my anxious self, the Joe I used to be.

To see this core of health and love, we must see it in ourselves first. For only in identifying and accepting our True Self are we able to forgive and see our own innocence. When we get caught up in fear, we tend to revert to the ego habits of jealousy, anger, hurt, competitiveness, having to be right, and so on. Seeing life through the filter of the ego's thought system becomes a self-fulfilling and self-validating reality. We tend to see in others — and everything in life — what we have already prejudged or come to expect. If we do this to our mate, we will sustain the ego's perception rather than seeing him or her fresh through the insight of the True Self.

Forgiveness

An inability to forgive is what prevents or destroys many relationships. What are the principles behind forgiveness? Think of resentment and guilt as a dam in a river. When the river of life is dammed up, it can't flow freely and it catches all the debris and pollution, contaminating the water. Forgiveness is opening the dam and letting the power of love and clarity return the river to its natural flow. When we forgive, we remove the dam that blocks our feelings of love and well-being.

No matter how well intentioned we are, we are all human and at times we succumb to the habits of our personalities, our past, and our fears. It is inevitable that a day will come (or it could be many times a day if we are tired) when — overwhelmed with life, feeling sick, or just caught up in a busy mind — we go unconscious and our ego self takes over. It can happen to any of us at any time. For many, it is a lifestyle to live at the mercy of our egos.

Forgiveness of our partner or ourselves is what allows us to reboot, and recover our health, our bearings, our sense of Self. Forgiveness opens us so that we drop our negative emotions of bitterness, anger, guilt, or resentment, and allow our feelings of true love to surface.

How do we forgive? I wrote about this in my book *Slowing Down to the Speed of Love*, and I will try to briefly summarize my key points here.

First, see the value of forgiveness. You must realize that the main person suffering from the lack of forgiveness is you. It is in your best interests to forgive because until you do your heart is closed. Like the plant that needs sunlight to live, the heart needs love.

Second, be willing to forgive. Willingness doesn't mean you can will yourself to forgive, it simply means you are open to forgive and have planted the seed for forgiveness to occur. Forgiveness comes with a change of heart but all the willpower in the world will not cause a change of heart. Still, even a little willingness will open the heart to a change.

Third, you can notice when you are not forgiving and when thoughts and feelings of resentment come to mind. Noticing those thoughts and choosing to simply observe them and not fuel them with more thoughts and attention allows the negativity to subside. Recognizing your unforgiving feelings as *thoughts* rather than as *a reality* allows you to see that you are re-creating those feelings now through the power of thought. This realization is not about denial or suppression; it's simply a matter of not engaging in past thoughts that might throw gas on the fire. Don't deny your feelings; be aware of them, accept them, and be willing to move on. Awareness, acceptance, and choice are the keys to transformation that leads to forgiveness.

Fourth, see the innocence of the other person or yourself. Seeing the innocence of another doesn't mean you don't hold them accountable for their actions and the consequences of those actions. What it means is that you stop the feeling of judgment that is blocking your love by understanding that every human being is doing the best they can at the level of awareness they are having in the moment. If they saw what they were doing from a higher level of conscious awareness, they would not have done what they did. This is true of all of us. If we actually realized when we were hurting another person that we were really hurting ourselves, we wouldn't do it. Realizing this fact of the human condition allows us to see their innocence as well as our own. Whenever I have had a change of heart and forgiven another, it has always come with seeing the other person's innocence — that they were doing the best they knew how at the moment.

Fifth, accept where you are in the moment if you are still feeling resentment or guilt. Don't judge yourself for not being able to forgive. Judging yourself will only slow the process of a change of heart and forgiveness. Acceptance with the awareness that you are willing to forgive and that it will happen in its own time allows us to manage until we have a change of heart.

A change of heart will come — and with it the return of the feeling of love — when we are willing to forgive; when we realize that our thoughts create our experience of resentment and guilt and we are able to choose the perspective of our True Self; when we see the innocence of the other person; and lastly, when we accept our innocence when negative feelings arise.

A Return to True Love

In relationships, falling "in love" reveals the essence of our being. When we feel that love within, we can't help but give it away to others. For it is in giving that we receive. In giving love, we experience the love as it comes through us, and in so doing, it becomes its own reward.

When we give love that comes from the heart, it is un-conditional. It is not giving in order to receive, with expectations and disappointments that follow, but giving because we are living in love.

If you discover this secret truth of love, you will have found how to sustain true love. If you realize this simple truth, you will remove fear from your marriage and with it all the fruits of fear — jealousy, envy, anger, resentment, neediness, possessiveness, thoughtlessness, and loneliness. Return to the love that is within you and you will be that river of love flowing out from your heart. It will return to you in countless ways.

Throughout the past twenty-nine years of our marriage, Michael and I have had our ups and downs as any couple does. Even when times were difficult for us personally or in our relationship, we were committed to our path back to love. At times I would take our love for granted, assuming it would always be there, and I'd fall back into the unconscious habits of my ego. Insidiously, the weeds of negativity and habits would creep in and cover up the plant of love, obscuring its beauty and joy. When I lost touch with my True Self, my feelings were always there to remind me and guide me back to love. Now, when I feel insecure, judgmental, empty, bothered, or bored with the relationship, I know it's time to tend the plant of love. We can count on our feelings as a guidance system to let us know when we have chosen fear vs. love, our ego habits vs. our True Self.

Knowing that I am off the path of love, the first choice I must make is to go within to my True Self and rediscover the treasure of love in me that has become obscured with thoughts — of things to do, and concerns about the world, family, finances, the normal distractions of our lives.

If I look to Michael to fix me or fill me up with love from the outside, the result is a feeling of neediness, control, and pressure, and that never works to return me to love. I have found that love is within, and when I am connected to my essence I can then see clearly the love that is all around me in those I love.

True love is a choice we must make — to look within and discover the love that we are. Once we return to love, we fall in love all over again with our partner and with life.

NAVA ATLAS is the distinguished author and illustrator of many books on vegetarian cooking, including the classic *Vegetariana, Vegan Express,* and *Vegan Soups and Hearty Stews for All Seasons.* In addition to cookbooks, articles, and an award-winning Web site (vegkitchen.com), Nava Atlas also produces visual books on family themes, humor, and women's issues. Her book, *Secret Recipes for the Modern Wife,* is a satiric look at contemporary marriage and motherhood through the lens of a faux 1950s cookbook. Atlas is also an active fine artist whose work is shown and collected by museums and universities across the United States.

SECRET RECIPES FOR A
SUCCESSFUL MARRIAGE

Nava Atlas

A few years ago, a wayward wisdom tooth snowballed into a full-blown dental emergency. I was warned that during oral surgery I would be under general anesthesia for quite some time, and might wake up with my jaw wired shut. Being a healthy person, and squeamish about medical procedures, my imagination ran amok — what if I died during surgery? I told my husband that should anything happen to me during this complex extraction, he had my permission to marry any one of my friends who were divorced or in the process. I was only half-joking; he was not amused. Still, beset by panic at my forthcoming surgery, I persisted; ticking my available friends' names off on my fingers, I soon ran out of digits.

I was left astonished at the sheer number of women I knew at the time whose marriages were dissolving. It seemed that some of the tales I'd been hearing about unraveling marriages were the stuff of sensational novels and movies. Other marital dissolutions were less dramatic. Persistent incompatibility, changes in circumstances, economic and family issues, and shifting goals or identities conspire to challenge an institution that, despite its purported fragility, remains a cornerstone of most cultures. As the date of surgery approached, pondering the tribulations of several close friends served as a distraction as I careened toward certain death, or at least an immovable jaw.

Obviously, I didn't die, nor was my jaw wired shut. The oral surgery was in itself successful and left me with two lasting effects: a painful neck injury, and an idea for a book, which became *Secret Recipes for the Modern Wife*. The latter was far more pleasant and profitable. A cookbook author by profession, I cooked up universal stories of marital issues into faux "recipes," accompanied by ghastly photos of 1950s food. These pairings served as metaphors for the various stages of marriage, from the addled bliss of engagement, to the falling in love with one's children, to the realization that once life throws its inevitable obstacles in your path, marriage tends to resemble a motley potluck rather than a delectable gourmet meal.

Certainly, not everyone I knew at the time of my oral surgery epiphany was breaking up. And we all know lots of couples who are going the distance, more by accepting and weathering life's ups and downs as a team than by buying into the myth of everlasting happiness. I planned to keep my beloved hubby of many years (and still do) even as I made my glib suggestion that he choose one of my friends in case of my demise. But in an odd way, I meant it, as I couldn't stand the thought of him being alone, uncoupled.

Our culture focuses far more on planning weddings than preparing for a lifelong partnership. I posit that ridiculously unrealistic expectations bear greater responsibility for potential disappointment than the institution itself. That's at the heart of what I comment on in my darkly humorous "recipes" and why my favorites are in the hopeful final chapter, which presents formulas for perseverance, patience, and even enduring romance. And it doesn't hurt to top everything off with a rich, homemade sauce of love, perspective, and a sense of humor — which in the long run is more palatable than sugarcoated fantasies.

Recipes on next page.

Happily-Ever-After Ambrosia

Serves to inspire hope in an age of cynicism

The stuff that makes marriage most delectable (choose as many as you'd like), including:

Shavings of fresh coconut
Harmony
Pineapple rings and candied fruit
Affection and mutual respect
Glistening cubes of ruby red gelatin
Security and support
Mint ice cream
Children that turn out well
Rich frosting and whipped cream toppings
Lasting love and happiness
Chocolate syrup (lots of it)

Before starting this recipe, recognize that even in an age when impossible standards of perfection coexist with a decline in marital rates (and successes), there must be *some* reason why most people aspire to be part of a committed couple.

While arranging delicious ingredients with lofty aspirations, pause to reflect on "for better or worse," and decide that you prefer better. And observe that even those who have endured the most painful of breakups often try again (and sometimes yet again).

Realize that real life doesn't always resemble a dessert buffet, filled with sensuous pleasures and emotional fulfillment. Still, it's human nature to feel hopeful, and even though you know that "happily ever after" exists primarily in fairy tales, it may be possible to grab morsels of love and happiness from time to time.

A Fairly Satisfactory Family Stew

Serves those who can endure the effort of preparation

2 large tear-inducing onions, finely chopped
Effort, as required
Olive oil
Ambivalence, as it arises
1 large pinch of perspective
Family-sized package of patience
Love, as needed
Biscuits for added coziness

While chopping the onions, weep a few tears of frustration as you exert the effort required to cook this complex stew of family life—the one you've created with your partner, and the families you joined together.

Ask yourself if you're up to the task of doing the hard work involved in concocting a flavorful, functional family stew, or if you want to continue your life as an aging party girl or an arrested adolescent.

Inhale deeply the savory scent of the onions as they cook in olive oil, becoming less bitter and stinging, and far sweeter and softer with time. As your weeping subsides, acknowledge lingering ambivalence about some of your main ingredients (including your husband, and even your kids, who might actually be more palatable if they were breaded and baked).

With a good pinch of perspective, come to accept that it can be quite satisfying to weather the peaks and valleys of seeing through such a challenging recipe, and that with patience, it may yield many tasty meals for years to come. Allow the stew to bubble along for as long as need be, and serve by the ladleful with love and biscuits.

For the past twenty years, JOHN VAN EPP, PH.D., has conducted numerous seminars and workshops on marriage, family, recovery, and divorce. He has developed a popular curriculum called PICK (Premarital Interpersonal Choices & Knowledge) a Partner, which is being taught in seven countries and forty-five states by hundreds of churches, organizations, educational settings, and agencies. He is the author of two books: *How to Avoid Marrying a Jerk* and *How to Avoid Falling in Love with a Jerk*.

The Healthy Imbalanced Marriage

John Van Epp, Ph.D.

Just the other day my wife, Shirley, told me how much she loves me and misses me. It was when the UPS driver came to the door and I jumped up and said, "Oh, don't let him leave — I need to talk with him." And Shirley mumbled under her breath, "Isn't he lucky to get a bit of time with you to talk."

Now some of you may think that an offhanded remark like that is a criticism. But I know that it comes from a heart of love that is just struggling with the insanity of a hectic schedule that has squeezed out all of our time to just be together, talking . . . planning . . . thinking out loud . . . and catching up with what has been happening in each of our lives. Let me explain.

We knew that this period of time was going to be stressful because we had just revised seven workbooks used in my two relationship courses and I needed to update the 350 pages of lesson plans and the power points and redo the twenty-some hours of filming to now match the new changes. All of this needed to be done yesterday in order to have a smooth transition from the previous edition to the new one, and we were all geared up to meet the challenge. But then a couple of unforeseen events occurred that took our stress to an entirely new level.

First, our youngest daughter (twenty-three years old) was diagnosed with three pulmonary embolisms and hospitalized for two weeks. We thank God that she is alive — and healing beautifully. But then a week later my stepmom passed away unexpectedly in her sleep. In spite of a total of nine bypasses and eleven stints since the 1980s, she had been vibrant and active at age eighty-six. Eight out of the nine siblings and their families converged within a week to mourn this loss. We hosted a number of our out-of-town family members and then provided a memorial dinner for forty in our home. Needless to say, it had been a very exhausting and emotional month for all of us, with little time for Shirley and me to just be alone together.

But isn't it fortunate that unpredictable times like this are few and far between . . . NOT! I think of the tagline — "Life comes at you fast" — and find myself echoing those words as I slow down and life seems to speed up. I have become convinced that being balanced is an illusion. Rest assured that in your marriage there is no perfect balance that you attain and then enjoy for the next fifty years. Just about the time you feel that you have a routine that is working in your relationship . . . life comes at you fast. Couples who are able to maintain a strong and close relationship over the rocky terrain of life don't accomplish this by achieving some higher order, balanced state that immunizes them from the ills of the world.

I can say this confidently: no one is truly balanced. I would not be surprised if many of you have just breathed your first sigh of relief at the thought that it is normal to be imbalanced. I must admit, I too found relief in accepting that life — and my marriage — is never balanced. Healthy marriages are not balanced relationships, rather, they're about *balancing*. You see, the key to success in your marriage is ultimately found in your commitment to regularly balance your imbalances.

It is normal to become imbalanced. It is normal that Shirley and I had three unrelated but overwhelmingly emotional and stressful situations happen at the same time (it is so common that there is an old saying that "bad things come in threes"). It would have been impossible to stay "balanced" in our time together, our communication, our romance, and most every other area of our relationship over the last couple of months. We became imbalanced. That is normal. It is not bad.

But what is dangerous is when little imbalances do not become realigned. As soon as you stop balancing, you put yourself at risk of becoming stuck in a lifelong rut where important needs and relationship experiences are neglected. In time, these overlooked imbalances become slow leaks in the closeness and strength of your bond. And your bond is the glue that holds the pieces of your marriage and family together.

Everett Worthington, Ph.D., is the professor and chair of the Department of Psychology at Virginia Commonwealth University and has been on the faculty since 1978. He has published seventeen books and over 150 articles and scholarly chapters, mostly on forgiveness, marriage, and family topics. In "Repairing the Emotional Bond: Marriage Research from 1997 through Early 2005," which appeared in the *Journal of Psychology and Christianity,* Vol. 24, No. 3, Worthington concludes that "beneath these [research] findings, we discover the buried treasure. The emotional bond between couples is the golden thread that holds partners together. Marital success is NOT most importantly about how partners behave with each other. It is MORE about the emotional bond between them and about healing threats to that bond." Frequently balancing the bond of your relationship is the key to your success in marriage.

I have been conducting marriage counseling for over twenty-five years. What amazes me is the large number of couples who have never been taught or even tried to develop a plan to regularly balance their relationship bond. For most, this is a very abstract concept comparable to running a financial budget or checking calendars. I have seen some couples who are natural relationship managers, and they practice the art of regularly balancing their bond without a formal plan or even any awareness of what they are doing right. However, these couples represent a very small minority of the overall number of marriages. So I would like to suggest that you have frequent huddles, weekly or monthly, but on a very consistent basis where you realign the imbalances of your marriage and set goals to strengthen your bonds of love.

I developed a model of a relationship bond in 1985 that I have since used in teaching graduate coursework, counseling, developing curricula, and writing. The model is the Relationship Attachment Model (RAM), (see Figure 1 below), and it portrays five major relationship bonds that contribute to the overall relationship

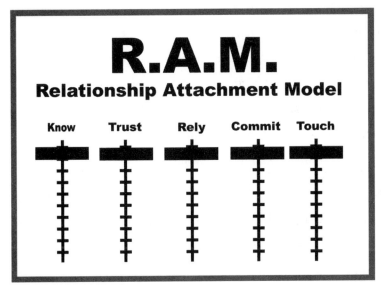

Figure 1

bond. It is a visual, interactive model that can easily depict both a balanced relationship as well as a relationship that is out of balance. If the truth be known, relationships are complicated. It is no wonder most couples do not think about managing their relationship bond . . . what is that?!? That is why a model that visualizes the five strands that are braided together to form the overall relationship cord will be so helpful and empowering to you. You can think of each one as a specific relationship connection that contributes to the overall or global bond in your relationship.

Let me explain each of these five strands and then suggest a way that you can use this model to regularly balance your relationship. The first bonding strand is the degree to which you know your partner. Your first reaction may be, "What are you talking about? I know my partner." But I am referring to the way you share your thoughts, dreams, feelings, and experiences from day to day — so that you can truthfully say, "My partner knows me better than anyone else." This kind of knowing requires quality communication, but it also necessitates enough quantity of time together to move from surface chitchat to more meaningful sharing.

Obviously, this level has dropped significantly over the last month and a half in my marriage. It creates mixed feelings and makes the relationship feel out of sync. And even though it is normal that life sometimes steals the time needed to keep our connection strong, it is essential that my wife and I make a plan to balance this imbalance.

The second bonding strand is the trust you have for your partner. Most of you will immediately think that trust only refers to staying faithful. But trust actually involves so much more. Trust is a feeling of confidence and security that comes from your belief in your partner. This belief can be compared to a picture in your head. In other words, as you have grown to know your partner, you have formed a dynamic image that's influenced by what you really think of your partner, including your expectations, interpretations, and attitudes.

I think it is fair to say that you live with two partners — the partner in your home and the partner in your head! They are not always the same. But the one in your head is certainly the most influential in your emotional bond. In fact, you can sometimes become stuck in a bad attitude, especially when an irritation has festered into a deep resentment that seems to color all you see. At that point, your partner may do something wonderful, but the picture in your head acts like a lens that distorts the way you see your partner. This is an example of a lowered trust level on the RAM.

I clearly remember (with a bit of embarrassment) a time early in our marriage when my distorted "trust-picture" of Shirley caused me to read a situation completely wrong. We had been married five years and our firstborn, Morgan, was close to turning three. I had a very important engagement to attend that summer but only had enough time to leave my office, pick up Shirley and Morgan, drop Morgan at the sitter's house, and head to the appointment. I knew that I could escape from my office on time, but I was worried that Shirley would not be ready when I arrived home, since during this time, Shirley was often late — of course, a toddler in diapers certainly didn't help.

I decided to check in around lunchtime and see how things were progressing. I couldn't tell her that I was worried — that would be insulting. So I called to "just see how her day was going." She told me that she was about to give Morgan a bath, and then she would be getting ready herself. I appreciated the unprompted reassurance.

But it was on the drive home that the Shirley in my head began to haunt me. I found myself imagining worst-case scenarios, wondering what I would say. And before I knew it, I was holding entire imaginary conversations with my wife who was a half hour behind schedule. I tried to shake these disturbing images and reassure myself that Shirley certainly knew how important this event was and that we simply could not be late.

As I pulled up our driveway, the front door flew open and Morgan came running towards me, her arms stretched outright, laughing and yelling, "Daddy's home." It was a hallmark moment . . . except for one thing — she was butt-naked. As I carried her into the house, it was as if life shifted into slow motion. I rounded the corner to find Shirley still in her bathrobe with green mask all over her face. My worst nightmare had come true. In order to not create a scene I asked what I could do to help her get ready to go. She gave me this puzzled look. "To the meeting!" I exclaimed. She then realized what I was referring to and explained, "They called and moved it to next week — they said they were going to also call you at the office so I just figured you knew."

I must confess that I did not come clean with Shirley that day. I think I said something like, "I knew something happened because you definitely would have been ready!" However, years later I told this story in a presentation, overlooking the fact that Shirley was in the audience. Afterwards she came up to me and, with a smile, prodded, "Do you have something more to say . . . ?" I quickly apologized and we had a good laugh.

Keeping a good attitude toward your partner is vital for maintaining a healthy dose of trust and respect in your relationship. Two other skills are needed to strengthen trust after it has been bruised or seriously broken: forgiving and rebuilding a belief in your partner. These skills can be learned and developed. But I should also emphasize that trust is not a gift — it is earned.

This leads us to reliance, the third bonding strand in the Relationship Attachment Model. Reliance refers to the ways that you meet each other's needs, divide your responsibilities and work together to fulfill them, and engage in meaningful and enjoyable experiences. For the past ten years, when teaching the session on reliance in my LINKS course, I always divide the couples into two groups (men and women) and have them generate a top ten list of what husbands and wives want from their partners. The twist comes when I ask the women to brainstorm what husbands want from their wives, and ask the men to figure out what wives want from their husbands. You should try this in your first huddle — you'll be amazed how this activity reveals what you need to be doing to best meet the needs and wants of your partner.

The fourth bonding strand is your commitment. Some of you may think that commitment was only the vows you made at the altar. But think of commitment as carrying your partner in your heart, so that wherever you are, regardless of the separation of time and space, your partner is there too. Commitment says, "I belong to you and you belong to me. Where you go, I will be there." Commitment, then, is practicing the presence of your partner. Regularly exercising your commitment strengthens the spirit of your resiliency, which will hold you together when life depletes any or all of the other four links of the RAM.

And the fifth bonding strand in the RAM is your sexual touch. Your romance, flirting, chemistry, and entire sexual relationship is a major source of closeness and intimacy. Even the chemicals that are produced in your brain (oxytocin, dopamine, and vasopressin, to name a few) are known for their bonding and addicting effects. Sex is bonding, whether it is a quickie or a night of passion.

The RAM provides a picture of your relationship and the five major sources of your feelings of closeness and bonding. But don't think it is only my life that gets out of balance. The normal course of your marriage is to encounter the unexpected, which will lower one or more levels of the RAM in your relationship. If you just imagine one of the levels of the RAM dropping to halfway, what effect do you think this would have on the other four links? Of course, it would pull them down also. Therefore, each strand is independent of the others but interacts in very dynamic ways. Vulnerabilities develop below the surface whenever an imbalance continues without you and your partner addressing it. These vulnerabilities are like underground faults. They can go undetected for long periods of time until an increase of pressure activates the fault and rocks your marriage.

This is why you must have regular huddles. There are four easy steps to your huddle, and each step applies a bonding strand of the RAM. When you sit down together and agree to have your huddle, step one involves asking yourselves how you both have been doing in the last few weeks to a month in your communication. Have you been talking enough? Are there topics or issues that you need to find some time to talk about? How have you been talking to each other? How have you been listening? Is there anything you want to change or improve before your next huddle?

Many couples like to do step two before step one. This step applies the important skills that strengthen your trust. Both of you express what you love and appreciate about each other — especially since your last huddle (of the previous week or month). Take a significant amount of time to do this. Do not rush.

The importance of expressing your love and appreciation to your spouse in positive actions and words has been the conclusion of much of Dr. John Gottman's research in his love lab in Seattle, Washington. Dr. Gottman has observed and studied couples' microexpressions for over three decades. As he states in *The Seven Principles for Making Marriage Work*, he can predict, with more than 90 percent accuracy, which couples will stay together and which ones will break up within the next three years. The key to making the prediction is the ratio of positive to negative interactions. In other words, positive interactions reveal (and develop) the strength of the bond in your relationship. Every huddle should be saturated with verbal and nonverbal expressions of appreciation, affirmation, and love.

Step three applies the "reliance" bonding strand to your huddle agenda. Look at how you have been working together and meeting each other's needs. Take your top ten lists and see what you did together and what you did not have time to do last month. Ask yourselves, what should we plan on doing together this next month that will make us feel closer, more balanced? Be sure to include your romantic and sexual relationship in this third step (which could transform your huddle to a cuddle).

The last step is the action step. It is when you look at your schedule, BlackBerry,® and any other calendar you use, and set some goals from the first three steps and schedule them to be implemented by specific dates. It is too often that you say you are going to do something but never get around to ever making it happen. Not with your huddle. You always have to translate what resulted from the first three steps — how you are doing in your talk time, your attitudes of trust and respect, and your togetherness — into a commitment. Putting these things on your calendar will greatly increase your success rate with balancing your imbalances.

Imagine this. You begin to have your huddle on a regular schedule — for some of you it is weekly and others once a month. But for all, you make this huddle a ritual in your marriage. You follow the four steps and use the RAM to help visualize where you are in the bonds of your relationship. You set goals that you want to accomplish before the next huddle. Just think what your relationship would be like after two years of consistently having huddles! No matter what your marriage is like today, it can only get better with regular huddles. Know this — your relationship will not run itself. You must run your relationship. The RAM provides a simple yet comprehensive plan for balancing your imbalances and keeping strong the bonds of your love.

LINDSEY RIETZSCH is the author of the practical, entertaining book *How to Date Your Spouse*. A former employment counselor for the state of Utah, she has worked as a certified instructor for the Department of Workforce Services, teaching assertive communication and job retention skills. Rietzsch has been an instructor and has designed curriculum for self-management and relationship courses. Her "How to Date Your Spouse" class was the inspiration behind her book of the same title. She is a motivational speaker on the topic of relationships and self-improvement and is currently coproducing a *How to Date Your Spouse* DVD.

Love as a Lifestyle

Lindsey Rietzsch

As a child I had a vague view of what happy marriages were. My parents fought like cats and dogs and eventually divorced when I was eight years old. The relationships they entered into with others down the road were no different. I knew that marriage didn't have to be that way and promised myself that when I married someday, I would do everything to ensure that my husband and I were happy and in love.

My parents' examples are the backbone behind my wonderful marriage of nine years and counting to my sweet husband Manuel. Everything they didn't do in their marriage to make it work is the very core of the message I teach to couples all over the world today. Marriage is a lifelong journey full of ups and downs, twists and turns, rocky roads and speed bumps. In the United States 50 percent of all marriages end in divorce. With all the extra stresses that add to your marriage — such as the economy, kids, your job, and your health — it's easy to lose hope. So, how can you avoid being a statistic? It's simple; date your spouse.

Since publication of my book *How to Date Your Spouse*, I have often been asked by skeptics, "What does it mean to date your spouse?" I respond that there is more to dating than just the actual date itself — it's really a lifestyle.

Think back to when you were first "dating" your spouse. You were daily trying to convince him/her that you were the one. Yes, you were always on your best behavior and always trying to stay positive and likable. Good breath, nice hair, a fun sense of humor, and all the other factors that play into wooing a lover were a part of your daily regimen. You took the time to care about your spouse, putting his/her needs before your own, listening with intent, and holding hands. You loved the thought of being in his/her arms; and knowing your partner was at the center of your thoughts made you smile. This is what it means to "date" your spouse.

Remember when your heart would skip a beat when your sweetheart looked at you a certain way or paid you a surprise visit? Remember the flirting, silliness, humor, and playfulness in the beginning? Did you feel more youthful, free, and almost invincible at times? I'm sure you experienced a reality check when the bills and the kids came along. It was most likely reality that slowly eroded the giddiness and spark in your relationship, the way a downpour washes away a beautiful chalked sidewalk mural.

To have a healthy, happy, and enjoyable marriage is a choice. You may not be able to make choices for your spouse but you certainly can influence his/her decisions. By implementing the tactics you once applied while initially courting your spouse, the spark will come back and you'll quickly remind your sweetheart why he/she fell in love with you in the first place.

Here are seven factors in the date-your-spouse lifestyle that are key to getting back those lost butterflies.

"E" for Effort

Remember how exciting everything was when you first began dating? You and your "spouse-to-be" were always on your best behavior and always looking for ways to stay on cloud nine. You actually planned your dates ahead of time. Why? You wanted everything to be smooth and perfect. Being prepared and taking time to arrange a special night is a display of affection, love, and respect.

Things should not be any different now. Your partner will still feel special when you make an effort to clean the car before a romantic night on the town. As the date begins, leave behind any baggage from your busy day and focus on your spouse. Bring along a camera and take pictures. Be proud to be seen with your husband/ wife and make every moment count. By making your significant other feel important and special, the results will be anything but disappointing!

Earn Interest

When I first met my husband, Manuel, he was a customer who came into the print store I worked at. He was dressed in soccer attire and because he had an eight-year-old boy in tow, I assumed he was married and much older than he really was. As he began flirting with me, I began to feel bad for his poor wife who had no idea he had a wandering eye. I did not flirt back and hoped my professionalism would send a strong hint.

Later he returned dressed in regular clothes, wearing tantalizing cologne, and without the little boy at his side. I quickly learned we were the same age, attending the same university, and that he was a German foreign exchange student on an athletic scholarship and living with a host family who had an eight-year-old son. Suddenly I was interested in soccer, contemplated learning German, and became much more excited about going to school and work each day. As he paid surprise visits to my work and appeared on campus out of nowhere, offering to walk me to class, I loved the mystery and excitement of being pursued.

Everyone loves that feeling of being admired, especially by the person you've fallen head over heels for. Before you were married, you were extremely interested in every part of your sweetheart's life. What were his talents, who were her friends, where did he work, what were her favorite pastimes? There was something so exciting about unfolding these mysteries. When she was sad, you wanted to know why. When he was excited, you wanted all the details. It was this interest in each other's lives that created bonding experiences and connected the two of you together.

As you continue to date your spouse now, think of new questions to ask him/her. If old topics or stories are revisited, listen as though you are hearing them for the first time. Spend time with your spouse doing the things he/she loves to do. This will help you learn more about your spouse and why he/she loves to do these things. Try to see things from his/her perspective as often as possible. Love and appreciate your spouse for who he is today, not who he was when you first met or what you hoped he would become. By stepping into your spouse's world and expressing excitement or curiosity about the things he/she is passionate about, your spouse will develop a strong interest in your world as well.

Ignite the Romance

If you find that the romance has dried up, step back and evaluate your dating style. When you plan dates, are you arranging something romantic or special? Movies, dinner, recreational activities (especially with the kids) are always fun, however "fun" does not always invite romance. It's great for building a friendship, but what about a love life?

Plan dates that create a mood for this. Soft music, candles, and perfume never hurt. Also, anything that allows for you to be physically close with few distractions will help you to focus on each other and build that sense of romance. Dancing, ice skating, spa services, swimming, etc. are examples of activities that offer physical closeness and are free of stress and distractions.

Time and time again romance often gets overlooked and viewed as beating around the bush when some just want to "cut to the chase." Often men see romance as unnecessary while women yearn for it night and day. In my own marriage, my husband knows that romance is preparation for the climax. When a woman feels special, beautiful, her mate's number-one priority, it is easier for her to feel passionate about and in tune with her spouse's needs. Romance triggers an electric pull that influences a woman's desire to connect with her husband on a physical level. It's worth every effort to cultivate romance if you feel things are lacking in this department.

Rachel and her husband, Brett, had been married six years and had four children. You can imagine how quickly raising four young children can zap the romance right out of a marriage. For Brett and Rachel, that is exactly what happened. When they found the time and energy to go out together, it was usually nothing out of the ordinary, or anything special. Over time the excitement and passion began to dwindle. Rachel lost the desire to express physical intimacy as well as the desire to receive it. Sleep sounded much better than physical contact or anything that seemed like "work." Brett began to feel rejected and slowly distanced himself from his wife.

It wasn't until receiving a copy of *How to Date Your Spouse* that the lightbulb came on. The couple realized that they had not been doing anything that would draw them closer together and build intimacy. Yes, romance was a missing ingredient in their recipe for love. They began making changes, such as taking the time to plan date nights in advance, choosing fun and romantic themes, and changing their environments as often as possible. Between the exciting surprises, dressing up, trying new activities (such as taking ballroom classes), and building an atmosphere that welcomed flirting and romance, Rachel and Brett felt like they were connecting on a whole new level. It was as if they had just met for the first time and were learning new things about each other and exploring new horizons. Making that effort to plan romance into their dating activities truly made all the difference.

Dress to Impress

Smell good and dress attractively to entice your spouse to pursue a more intimate relationship. Visit a makeup counter or salon for a new, refreshing look. Purchase a new outfit to sport on your date. Take care of your body. You may be months away from your ideal weight or body image; however, just the act of exercising tells your spouse that you care about your body and want to be healthy and look your best. This is attractive in itself, as it builds good self-esteem, which is always a desirable characteristic.

My husband and I make it a habit to dress attractively no matter where we go. We want to feel good about ourselves and each other in public as well as at home. I feel proud to walk arm and arm with a good looking, nicely dressed partner. Manuel feels the same way. It's hard to lose your temper or think bad thoughts about someone you are very attracted to. Remember, this is a part of a lifestyle you are attaining, so it means attending to it on a daily basis.

Mystery Isn't History

Do you remember the first time you laid your eyes on your spouse? There was so much to unfold and you had so many questions. Every time you went out on a date, it was another opportunity to satisfy your curiosity. Why is it that years later you feel there is no more mystery left?

A positive way to build mystery back into your marriage is to plan surprises. Large or small, planning a surprise is a fun way to keep your spouse on his/her toes and wondering what you are up to. If your spouse is aware that you have a surprise in the works, it will be nearly impossible to keep it out of his/her mind. This means that you'll be the center of your spouse's thoughts.

Another great tip for adding a little mystery is to plan some healthy alone time for yourself. This allows for you to have a little bit of personal space, which is healthy for building a strong relationship. Even a weekend getaway with your close pals will allow for you to miss your spouse. Be sure to always take friends with you that your spouse approves of and who support your values. Never leave on an angry tone and make sure your spouse is okay with your absence. A great relationship booster if you have children is to put your spouse first and offer that he/she take a weekend off with friends while you watch the kids. A rejuvenated spouse comes with excellent benefits.

Fuel Excitement

Think back to when you last felt that butterfly sensation. Remember that it was an exciting feeling to have your heart start racing.

Adrenaline is the key component to this ultimate sensation of feeling head over heels in love. So how can you revisit this euphoric sensation? Plan some exciting dates with your spouse that will get your heart fluttering. Try something that you have avoided, such as skydiving, river rafting, skiing, or any adventure that makes you weak in the knees. Experiencing something new with your spouse that you have been afraid to try will obligate you to rely on him/her to help calm you down and keep you focused. Imagine freefalling on a bungee cord while being wrapped tightly in the arms of your spouse. What an exciting and euphoric feeling! This will work wonders for your marriage and create a date that you'll never forget.

Lydia and Dave were empty nesters experiencing a bit of a rut. They were caught in a routine of mundane weekend leisure with the same circle of friends and family. One night they fell deep into discussion about how they weren't getting any younger and should really be having the time of their lives now that the kids were gone. They decided to do something out of the ordinary and plan a month getaway to a place they had never been to nor had ever expressed any desire to visit. Not only were they going to surprise others by their unexpected choice, they would soon surprise themselves as they were determined to plan activities on their trip that were out of their typical comfort zone. Yes, New Zealand was the changing point of their relationship. Hiking waterfalls, kayaking, sailing, and ballooning were a big part of the couple's transformation — however, to this day they give full credit for the miraculous changes to just having the desire to "try something new."

Excitement doesn't always need to be life-risking feats. A fun concert, an amusement park, a game of flag football or anything that allows you to feel youthful and playful will trigger these feelings. A great alternative to getting back butterflies and euphoria via an adrenaline rush is to have a staring contest while in each other's arms. Set a small prize for the winner, such as choosing where to go for dinner or picking out the movie rental, etc. Try not to blink while those butterflies get busy!

Flirt!

Need I say more? If flirting feels foreign, then you have some work to do. Wrap your arms around your spouse often; be playful and youthful. It's okay to let loose and be silly once in a while. Don't be afraid to publicly praise and compliment each other. Yes, touchy-feely, lovey-dovey has its benefits. Be careful not to go overboard and overwhelm your spouse. Look for appropriate moments and find balance.

It feels good to love someone and it feels even better when that someone loves you back. As you apply these tips in your own relationship, you'll notice a difference in your marriage, your self-esteem, confidence, professional performance, role as a parent, and overall demeanor. Happy and healthy marriages truly are the key to a better world.

Getting back that spark and excitement in your relationship may take some time, so plan on being patient and dedicated.

Once it returns, be sure to maintain it on a daily basis. When dating becomes a lifestyle, a satisfying and successful marriage is the result.

SCOTT HALTZMAN, M.D., is a clinical assistant professor of psychiatry and human behavior at Alpert Medical School of Brown University and is a distinguished fellow of the American Psychiatric Association. He is author of *The Secrets of Happily Married Men* and *The Secrets of Happily Married Women* and *The Secrets of Happy Families*, which bestselling author Michael Gurian called "a beautiful book — timely, passionate, and powerful." He practices marriage therapy in Rhode Island, where he regularly enjoys scones with his wife and children.

Cooking Up a Rich and Fulfilling Marriage

Scott Haltzman, M.D.

The Chemistry of Love

Lately I've noticed some strong similarities between baking and marriage. Baking, it turns out, is all about chemistry. If you want a cookie to brown, add sugar. If you want a blueberry pie to hold together, add cornstarch. If you want bread to rise, add yeast. In fact, through the magic chemistry of baking — and by adding some extra butter and a ton of chocolate chips to the mix — my wife, Susan, turns scones (one of the world's most boring foods) into a near-orgasmic culinary experience.

I don't know much about baking, but I know a lot about marriage. Not just because my wife and I have entered into our third decade of the institution, but because I've dedicated the last dozen years of my psychiatry practice to researching, writing about, and teaching others about how to have great marriages. So when I thought about my goal of improving marriage, it was only natural that I saw the similarities to baking. You can bake a richer and more fulfilling scone the same way you can create a richer and more fulfilling marriage: by understanding the underlying basic chemistry, making the choice to add some ingredients, eliminate others, and put them all together in the right proportions.

When a couple meet each other and fall in love, they groove to the great feelings they generate together. If they make the decision to marry, they are convinced they have all the ingredients right from the start to keep them happily married forever. But they lose sight of an important law of human attraction: the ingredients that bring people to each other, and produce powerful feelings of desire, are not the same ingredients that keep couples together over the long run.

If we take a peek at some of the brain chemicals involved in the phases of love, we can see how things work themselves out. The hormones testosterone (high in men) and estrogen (high in women) can cause a couple to feel an initial sexual attraction. In many cases, though, after a fun night out, they may decide never to see each other again. The "What was I thinking?" event can be explained quite easily: you weren't thinking. It was your hormones making you act, and that's not enough to make a lasting relationship.

After the "attraction" hormones fade from your system, the "infatuation" hormones take over. This includes the neurochemical dopamine, which stimulates the brain and energizes your emotions. The effects of the brain chemicals involved in infatuation give you three clear messages: 1) "This person makes me feel good when

I'm with them," 2) "Without them I am lost!" and 3) "I want to spend my life with this person." In our culture, when two single adult people have this feeling and are free to make decisions for themselves, they choose to marry. If you're reading this chapter, the odds are you're one of those people.

Here's the rub. And it's a big one. The brain chemicals that get you this far into the relationship don't linger forever. You think they will. You believe that you and the crazy/beautiful person whom you smote (and who was smitten by you) will always share those feelings simply by being in each other's presence.

Knowing that the infatuation phase doesn't last forever is a daunting thought at first, and many couples don't want to believe it. I recall hearing from a rabbi who told me how two of his congregants quit his synagogue after he told them during their marriage ceremony that they will not always have an easy time. "That's not us!" they insisted. The fact is that it is them. It's all of us!

Bummer? Not really. In fact, the revelation that your chemical high doesn't last a lifetime can be a source of comfort to you. Now when you don't see fireworks every time your mate walks in the door, you don't have to rack your brain to figure out what went wrong. Nothing went wrong. This is the way marriage goes. When that passion begins to fade, you now have a choice: let it dry up and wither away, or take an active role in reviving the feelings.

If you do nothing, your marriage becomes like a dried and bitter

English scone. And really, who wants that? If you make some small adjustments and add certain key ingredients, your marriage can become as rich as my wife's chocolaty-buttery scones. But you have to know what adjustments to make and what ingredients to add.

The Right Marriage Ingredients

Let's talk about what you should add to the batter of your marriage to sweeten it up. We know from research that people crave positive reinforcement; they want to be told that they look good, act well, and think smartly. Your mate, for example, wants to see the smile on your face when he or she walks in the room, even if you're having a bad day. It will brighten up your spouse to see such a reaction from you. Think about how positive you try to stay in the workplace. Your boss may be ragging on you, or your office mate may be making annoying clicking sounds with his pen, but you maintain your cool, stay pleasant, and seek ways to get along. When you act upbeat, people are nice to you. On the other hand, they clam right up when they are put down, criticized, or ignored. Whether at the job or at home, treating someone with a cheerful and encouraging attitude boosts their spirits. They get more of what they want, and you get more of what you want.

That doesn't mean that your spouse won't do something annoying every now and then. When that happens, think of all the ways that you love them (hard work at the moment, I know!). Then, tell them something good about themselves. Now, if it's really important, you can point out what bothers you. Let's say, for example, that your husband leaves water on the floor after he bathes the kids. If you respond to the situation with this very accurate observation, "You're a thoughtless slob," the marriage won't get stronger. On the other hand, you'll get off to a much better start by saying, "I really think you're a great dad, and so much appreciate your bathing the kids. I know what hard work it is, and you do such a great job. I love how clean they smell afterward." But, you say, this suggested response doesn't even mention the wet floor! Right! Really, in the grand scale of things, does a little minor flooding matter? Yes! you say. Well, if it's that important, then you can mention the wet floor, but only after you praise his wonderful child-bathing technique. And when you do mention the problem, do so softly, as in, "I'm a little worried about the water on the floor after you finished. Do you think you could use a bath mat next time?" Trust me; it works better than calling him a slob.

Saying nice things is important, but doing nice things can also sweeten a marriage. Bring home flowers or take-out food when you come home from work. Send cards. Buy gifts for no reason whatsoever. And be sure to buy gifts for reasons also! Sometimes, loving acts can come in the form of cooking a meal or mowing the lawn. My wife loves when I take out a toothbrush and polish her jewelry. These small acts can make a big impact.

When you were dating, the excitement came to you automatically. Remember the electrifying chemical, dopamine, that flooded your brain when you fell in love with your guy or gal? Well, that chemical doesn't automatically sustain its high levels after you exchange rings; in fact, it tends to fade. But you can trick your body into pumping dopamine back into your brain, and it's fun to do. Together, involve yourselves in any stimulating or invigorating activity (inside and outside of the bedroom) and you'll share a surge of positive connection with each other. These activities can include taking a class together, going on a roller coaster ride, hiking in a park you've never been to before, geocaching in the woods, or eating at a new restaurant. People bond when they share thrilling events together, but those events don't happen if you fall into the same old routine. Do something different and feel some of that attraction start to grow.

Perhaps the greatest marriage booster is the gift of listening. We all think we listen. Even bad listeners think they listen well. But really good listeners have a trick, and here's what it is: they make sure that the speaker feels heard. They ask questions like, "Can you tell me more?" and "What do you mean by that?" They respond by saying, "Really!" and "Wow! That's interesting!" or "That sucks!" They try to collect as much information as the speaker wants to convey. And when the speaker is done, they make an effort to repeat back what the speaker said. By honest inquiry and reflecting back the information conveyed, a miracle in communication happens: the speaker feels heard!

There are things that good listeners don't do. Good listeners don't interrupt (unless they are seeking clarification) and they don't jump in with their point of view until after the speaker feels listened to. One of the most difficult things to do in marriage is to hold back the temptation to clarify or correct when our partner speaks. "But...but...you don't understand," you're tempted to sputter. Remember, in most cases your mate isn't talking to hear your opinion (hard to believe, I know) but because he or she has an opinion that is important for you to hear. If you get defensive, try to explain things away or, worse, try to point out why your mate's feelings are wrong, I can guarantee you, you'll have a bitter taste in your mouth after the interaction. Even if your loved one is mistaken, it's still better to make sure you hear the whole story first.

There are so many ingredients that will alter the outcome of your marriage. Think about all the positive attitudes and acts that you can mix into your relationship with your life partner. Then mix! Consider all the elements that drag down your marriage or add bitterness or hostility to it — and leave them out!

Creating a fabulous marriage is like creating a great scone. Make a few small changes, and the difference can last a lifetime.

JOEL CROHN, PH.D., is a clinical psychologist in private practice in San Rafael, California. He is a respected researcher and author who has lectured nationally about cross-cultural issues in love and work for over fifteen years. Dr. Crohn is also the acclaimed author of *Mixed Matches,* and coauthor of *Beyond the Chuppah: A Jewish Guide to Happy Marriages,* and *Fighting for Your Marriage.* His work has been featured frequently in the media, including *The Leeza Show, The Love Chronicles* (A&E), and the *San Francisco Chronicle.*

MIXED MATCHES:
CREATING SUCCESSFUL INTERRACIAL, INTERETHNIC, AND INTERFAITH RELATIONSHIPS

Joel Crohn, Ph.D.

Mixed matches are often very romantic relationships. The novelty of being with someone not like the boy or girl next door adds an element of excitement. Novelty is one of the spices of life, and its power can distract people from focusing on the ordinary problems that are part of every relationship.

When a relationship includes an element of forbidden love, the attraction can become even more powerful. Choosing a partner over the opposition of family, friends, or religious traditions can lead to an idealization of the relationship, at least initially. Each partner silently reflects that "If I have chosen her (or him) in spite of these obstacles, I must really be in love."

While lack of family acceptance can destabilize a cross-cultural relationship, it can also have the opposite effect. Cut off from the usual sources of support, the couple that feels exiled is figuratively pushed into one another's arms. Resenting the judgments of others, they focus their anger on their families and may fail to experience normal ambivalence about their new relationship. Like a nation threatened by enemies from without, they close ranks and temporarily forget their own differences.

Few couples want to disrupt the delicious experience of new love with disturbing thoughts of possible future problems. And who can blame them? Falling in love is one of the most sought after experiences in life, a magical emotional and sexual state of being. Frequently, part of falling in love includes the belief that we have found our true and unique soul mate. And if our beloved is from a background unlike our own, it may even reinforce the feeling of specialness, of having found our missing half. After all, how else can we explain these intense feelings?

There is only one problem with being head-over-heels in love. No matter how high up we start, we always come down. Time is the gravity of love. The intoxicating and delusional state of new love — that sense of finding the perfect other — never lasts.

The real test of a relationship comes when the bubble bursts. Whether it's over dealing with family rejection, planning a wedding, coping with a child's birth, making religious choices, or deciding who is supposed to wash the dishes, differences eventually emerge. New love ends, and couples are able to begin forging deep and solid relationships by acknowledging and dealing with their differences.

Don't be so attached to your fantasy relationship that you miss the opportunity to build a real one that will last.

Clarify Your Different Cultural Codes

Culture shapes every aspect of how we view the world and what we consider "normal" and "abnormal." It molds our attitudes towards time, family, sex, and monogamy. Cultural rules govern how we expect anger and affection to be expressed, the ways that children are supposed to be disciplined and rewarded, how we greet strangers and friends, and the roles of men and women. Behavior that I consider neighborly, you may define as seductive; what you intend to be friendly disagreement, I may be just as sure is a threat; when you say you visit your parents "often," you may mean twice a year, but for me "seldom" might mean twice a week. If we are not able to identify the existence and the nature of these differences in each other's cultural codes, we will have problems dealing with stressful situations.

Partners in a mixed match raised in different countries can have very different cultural definitions of "normal." Just imagine the potential value conflicts in an intermarriage between a Japanese man, from a culture where men average eleven minutes of housework a day, and an American woman, from a culture where men average 108 minutes of housework. Their expectations of what is "normal" are not likely to easily mesh.

Even when both partners in a mixed match are born in the same country, speak the same language, and are from the same class background, they may find themselves tripping over cultural differences in the meanings of words, behaviors, and values. Regional, ethnic, racial, and religious differences may lead two native-born partners from different subcultures to interpret the same action in very different ways. Differences in accents between one part of a country and another are usually obvious; contrasts in cultural codes often are not.

Consider, for example, a recent dispute between Adam, a Norwegian American man, and Serena, an Argentinean American woman. Both of them were the grandchildren of immigrants to the United States. Both were well educated. They had met in graduate school and shared many common interests. They cared deeply about each other, and it never occurred to them during the first year of their relationship that their different cultural conditioning might lead them to react very differently in stressful moments.

A seemingly minor incident revealed the different cultural lenses through which they each viewed the world. They were cooking dinner together one night at Adam's apartment. Serena's hands were wet and slippery, and she accidentally broke one of Adam's favorite bowls that had been handed down to him by his grandparents. Serena apologized profusely, and Adam told her not to worry about it. But in the hours that followed, he retreated into a silence Serena found unbearable.

Finally, she blew up. "I know you're upset, but you just don't say anything. I feel guilty enough about breaking the bowl, but your silence is really driving me crazy." Adam responded to her outburst with more silence to which Serena responded with even more anger. The incident sparked the first major fight they ever had, highlighting differences that they had only been subliminally aware of.

When they finally began to discuss what had happened, they began to see the contrast in the ways their families had dealt with conflict. Adam said that he felt being quiet was the way to keep the peace. He had never seen any direct expression of anger between his parents. For him, silence was the normal way to communicate feeling upset.

In Serena's much more expressive family, one of the ways that people demonstrated their sense of connection was through direct, and sometimes loud and angry, outbursts. If you were angry and didn't show it, it meant you didn't care. And since people cared about one another deeply in her family, recurrent anger was a normal and expected part of family life. She sensed Adam's irritation about the broken bowl, but to her his silence meant that he must not really care about their relationship. Her way of trying to reconnect was to demonstrate even more intense emotion to show how much she really cared about Adam.

It wasn't just that they had grown up in different families that led Serena and Adam to very different conclusions about what constituted normal and expected behavior; it was the differences in the entire social worlds they had experienced as children. Adam had grown up in a predominately Scandinavian/Lutheran neighborhood in Minneapolis. Serena had grown up in a neighborhood in a Miami suburb populated primarily by families from all over Latin America. The values and behavior inside the home were echoed and reinforced by their friends and in other social exchanges they experienced and observed. Until they went to college, each of them had had little opportunity or need to question their families' definition of normalcy.

Unfortunately, the contrasts in the cultural rules we bring to our relationships are usually invisible until they have been violated. We internalize the norms of our subculture as children and grow up taking them for granted. Therefore, when I get angry with your behavior, my first assumption is that you as an individual are behaving in an offensive manner, not that we are operating by two different sets of cultural rules. One of the most important tasks for partners in mixed matches is to learn to understand and deal with the differences in the cultural codes they bring to their relationship.

Sort Out Confusion About Your Identity

Whether we admit it or not, most of us carry around a mixed bag of contradictory feelings about our cultural, racial, or religious identities. In a rapidly changing, culturally diverse society, it's hard for anyone to maintain a clear and consistent sense of group identity. Our desire to melt into the melting pot is always at war with our wish to be a member of a distinct group. It's hard to have it both ways. Most of us at some time find ourselves struggling with inner confusion about where we fit culturally.

People who have experienced racism or religious persecution often feel that their group identification is an unwelcome burden. Those who have not suffered directly from discrimination in their own lives, but know of the victimization of their parents or grandparents, may wear their cultural label with ambivalence and anxiety. They may try to minimize or even obliterate their identity as a member of their group.

Even people from groups that have no memory of oppression may be ambivalent about their cultural identity. Their discomfort derives not from real or perceived external danger, but from an internal sense of incompatibility with their group. They may feel that their identity is "boring," or they may feel that their group's primary values do not fit well with their own.

But humans are profoundly social animals. We need to feel connected to a group. The group defines who is friend and who is enemy and provides a system of social support. Its norms help sort out priorities in a complex world.

So it should come as little surprise that so many people are strongly ambivalent about their connection to the identity inherited from their ancestors. The fact that membership in the group, be it African American, Jewish American, Asian American, Mexican American, or even New England Yankee, can be a source of support and emotional nurturance or can target us for the hostility of others means that we can experience group identity as a mixed blessing. And when either partner in a mixed match has conflicted feelings about his or her own racial, religious, or cultural identity, it can create confusion, conflict, and pain in a relationship.

Historically, identity as a member of a group was a matter of destiny, not decision. But as barriers have fallen, especially in the last twenty-five years, group identification has increasingly become a choice. We now face the complicated task of creating our own sense of identity. Like painters standing before a palate of colors, we can choose the shades and shapes of our identities. This can be both an exhilarating and a confusing task. By sorting out the complex feelings about your own group identity, you will be better able to compromise with your partner and find creative ways to synthesize your pasts.

Beyond Categories

It's not just the census bureau that likes to divide everything into as few neat and clean little boxes as possible. We are all tempted to reduce the complexity of life into the simplicity of either/or categories. At a certain primal level, we are comforted when we can clearly and unambiguously define people and situations as either one way or the other. He is either black or white, she is either right or wrong, they are either with us or against us. For at least a moment, we create order out of the chaos and uncertainty of life.

The problem isn't that we create categories. We have to. There is no way to deal with the overwhelming amount of information that bombards us every second without having ways of sorting it into a manageable number of cubbyholes. Our troubles begin when our categories become too rigid, and we begin to reject information that does not fit into them. That is when we begin to stereotype and distort the complexity of life in destructive ways.

Whether we are talking about racism, anti-Semitism, the hatred of one nation for the next, or a battle between lovers, we are inevitably dealing with the problem of inflexible and oversimplified categories. The great majority of human situations, especially those involving conflict, are more complicated than we would like to believe. The racist is usually no more receptive to information that contradicts his deeply held prejudices than the bitter husband is to reassurances about his wife's redeeming qualities. Most attempts at building bridges and resolving conflict have to deal with the problem of challenging stereotypes and overgeneralizations.

Married life sometimes seems, by its very design, to encourage spouses to reduce one another into two-dimensional stereotypes. Repetition, boredom, and, especially, the stress of raising children have a way of turning the exciting contrasts that were initially sources of attraction in a relationship into the focus of conflict. The words "you always" and "you never" are the danger signs that warn of rigid categories and of hardening hearts. But when people are able to relax their views of themselves and of their partners, to take risks, and to work to renew their bonds, they can create deep connections possible only in committed relationships.

AMANDA KANE, L.M.S.W., L.S.W., has gained recognition writing online and lecturing about an extensive range of psychological issues She is assistant director of psychological services at Fairleigh Dickinson University in Madison, New Jersey. Kane attended Vassar College and received a master of social work from Fordham University in New York City.

FIVE TACTICS FOR CREATING YOUR BEST MARRIAGE

Amanda Kane, L.S.W.

Whether you've been married for two months or twenty years, it is possible to create the marriage that you envision. For some couples this may require altering their present trajectory, while others may simply need to tweak an already solid relationship. Change is always possible, but it requires work. Challenging your marriage to evolve may at times feel unfamiliar or even uncomfortable. Transformation engenders many feelings — fear, excitement, and hope — to name just a few. It requires abandoning the old, safe dynamics and experimenting with something new and unknown. Change, much like marriage itself, requires risk and faith.

The most effective change is born out of personal reflection and targeted action. While every couple is special and every relationship has its strengths and weaknesses, the following tactics will help you to create your best marriage. It may be helpful to actually take out a paper and pen and write down responses to the following questions and suggestions. Writing is an invaluable therapeutic tool that helps to process and illuminate feelings.

Tactic #1: Design Your Ideal Marriage

What do you want from marriage? Often simple questions yield complex and important answers. It is difficult to create a satisfying union if you don't know what you really want out of it. Imagining the marriage of your dreams requires getting in touch with personal needs and longings. Some desires are reasonable and others are more irrational, but acknowledging basic yearnings gives us essential information about ourselves.

Various requirements may be practical. "I want a partner to help me raise the kids," or "I want someone to help with the housework." Other needs may be emotional. "I'd like a wife so that I don't feel lonely." "I want a husband to kiss me when I come home at night." The list is individual and limitless. Your list may include emotional needs, social needs, sexual needs, etc. Marriage, despite popular mythology on the subject, is not a one-size-fits all institution. Your ideal marriage may look much different than your neighbor's ideal marriage.

In the current incarnation of your marriage, are your basic relationship requirements being met? Ask yourself, "What would I like to change about my marriage? And, "What would I like to remain the same?" It may be difficult and even painful to acknowledge some relationship truths. However, think of these uncomfortable feelings as the fuel that motivates change. These questions and the resulting feelings are tools for exploration, which help evaluate your current relationship so that you can begin to visualize your ideal marriage.

It is vital to recognize that marriage should not be expected to meet every need. That would be too much to ask of a marriage, not to mention a spouse! Healthy lives are filled with many social connections — friends, coworkers, and family, who play vital yet complementary roles. Additionally, some needs are best fulfilled by a challenging career, an engaging passion, or devout spirituality — instead of a particular relationship. Introspection and journaling can yield crucial information about what you specifically want out of a marriage, as opposed to expecting it to arbitrarily fill various life voids. It is very possible that revamping a marriage also requires focusing other aspects of life that may have been neglected and attending to those simultaneously.

Self-understanding will allow you to live a more fulfilling life and will put you in touch with what you need from a life partner. Additionally, your pursuit of emotional consciousness may encourage your partner to also reflect on his or her relationship needs. Ideally, your spouse is open to the possibility of change and is open to expressing his or her desires. However, typically one partner is more eager for change than the other. If your spouse actively resists change, start paying close attention to what he or she is trying to communicate. Are they completely fulfilled by the relationship? Is it fear of the unknown? One of the best methods for finding answers is learning to listen.

Tactic #2: Listen with Your Heart

Communicating — whether speaking or listening — is not always easy! It takes practice to really hear what your partner is communicating. Therapists love to talk about the importance of communication but frequently minimize how difficult it can be to communicate about the really important things. Reminding your spouse to pick up milk at the grocery store is easier to utter than openly discussing raw emotional needs. It is perfectly normal to expect some discomfort when you are verbalizing emotionally loaded material. Uncomfortable feelings are probably a sign that you are outside your comfort zone and pushing yourself. Resist becoming overly engrossed in your feelings to the exclusion of your partner's perspective. It is crucial to hear where the other person in coming from. This is especially difficult, but you can, with practice, become a more attuned listener.

Listening is a frequently undervalued communication skill. The concept of "active listening" is critical to building your ideal marriage. Active listening involves focusing on the person speaking and letting go — ever so slightly — of your perspective and stake in the conversation. The best active listening has an element of empathy. The listener quiets his or her own ego and focuses all senses on the speaker. Tune into your partner's tone of voice and body language, as well as his or her words. Empathy allows one person's emotional state to resonate within another, and is essential for the kind of deep understanding that comes from the heart.

Attuned listening is an all-access pass to your spouse's inner world. It will help you to better know your spouse, and it will serve as a bridge when you disagree.

Tactic #3: Express Anger Responsibly

Anger is an emotion that gets a bad rap, especially in relationships. From an early age, many of us are taught to suppress, repress, or ignore our anger altogether. Culture says, "Don't be angry" or "Just get over it." Anger is frequently invalidated by feelings of guilt. "I shouldn't feel angry." This is unfortunate because anger is a completely valid emotion, which is rich with information. Feeling angry is a clear indication that something is not working. Anger sometimes pushes us to act impulsively, but anger is often best used as a tool for reflection. Try to sit with your anger and listen to what it is telling you.

The next time you feel angry at your partner, take some time out to journal. Stream-of-consciousness writing can reveal interesting and unexpected material. Or try something more structured and jot down your feelings (you may be feeling more than just anger) as well as information about the situation. Do you notice any patterns? Is this a relationship dynamic that emerges time and time again? How did your parents express anger? What did you learn about the emotion as a child? Exploring your history with anger will reveal helpful information that may clarify your current feelings.

Understanding your anger, like being in touch with your

relationship needs, provides vital self-knowledge, which can then be used to improve communication with your partner. Communication takes many forms — words, actions, even body language. Why is it so important to relationships? Communication lets your partner into your inner world — feelings, needs, expectations, disappointments, etc. Lack of communication closes our partner out and prevents intimacy.

Communicating anger effectively is one of the most necessary and difficult relationship skills. Managing anger can be tricky. Anger is an intense, sometimes unpleasant emotion that can be damaging when expressed thoughtlessly. Responsibly communicating anger involves knowing what not to say. Most of us have said something in anger that we later regret. Unfortunately, once words are spoken, they cannot be taken back. It is imperative to reflect before speaking, especially when emotions are raw. If you feel yourself becoming overwhelmed by anger, take thirty seconds to collect yourself before you say or do anything. It is important to honor feelings of anger without becoming injurious or abusive.

Not everyone lashes out when they are angry, and more passive-aggressive forms of anger can be equally harmful to relationships. Passive anger is the indirect expression of the emotion. (A husband, gritting his teeth, tells his wife, "Oh, no, I'm not angry," and then proceeds to complain about her to a coworker.) Expressing anger in this style can sabotage the couple's ability to address the problem directly (there isn't a "problem," remember?). Over time, unaired grievances build up and solidify into resentment. This erodes intimacy and sours love. Directly addressing the anger and working constructively to rebuild intimacy are the anecdotes for relationship damage. One of the most effective strategies for fortifying love is setting aside special time to reconnect.

Tactic #4: Create Sacred Time Together

Too often the business of everyday life prevents couples from investing in the work it takes to maintain a satisfying marriage. Think of a marriage like a joint bank account. The couple makes deposits in the form of time, energy, attention, caring, and support, among other intangibles. Withdrawals take the form of taking each other for granted, saying something thoughtless when you're tired, "forgetting" to make love for weeks at a time — you get the idea. In order to maintain equilibrium, you don't want to only withdraw from the account. Both partners need to work to increase the balance on all the good things that equalize the withdrawals. Problems emerge (overdraft!) if couples constantly make withdrawals, or if one person takes and takes without giving back to the other.

A simple tactic for adding to your relationship balance sheet is with sacred time together. This can be anything that is special and energizing for you and your spouse. Date nights, daily walks in the evenings, salsa lessons together, or anything that you both enjoy qualify as deposits. The time is sacred because, forgoing an emergency, you make it a real priority. The specific activity isn't as crucial as the mere fact that you are both setting aside this special time for yourselves. Prioritizing this sacred time communicates that the marriage is important to both partners. It also carves out a space for spouses to bond and remember why they got together in the beginning.

Sacred time together nurtures the needs of the marriage. Your marriage is a separate entity apart from yourself or your mate. A marriage reflects the needs and boundaries of two people. It has its own requirements, which probably don't always align with your individual desires. You may have to give up your book club on Tuesday if that is the only day of the week when your wife can meet for a date night. It takes compromise and work to protect marriage from general intrusions such as kids, jobs, in-laws, and other responsibilities.

Sex is an additional component of sacred time together. The sexual aspect of marriage is partially what defines it and sets it apart from other relationships. Sexual engagement is incredibly important in a marriage. Prioritizing sex is no easy task, given everyone's busy lives, but it is vital for relationship survival over the long haul. Enjoying sex with your partner is also crucial. Frequently couples drift apart sexually and do not know how to find the desire that they once shared. Connecting with each other through other special, enjoyable activities can help start the process. Beginning to talk about the problem is another fundamental intervention. Discussing something so intimate can be especially emotional, leading many wise couples to seek the guidance of a therapist.

Tactic #5: Keep Love in the Foreground

It is all too easy to focus on relationship problems and then forget about what brought you together in the first place. Maybe your husband dropped his morning coffee on the new carpet, or maybe your wife forgot to buy you lactose-free milk at the grocery store. All relationships are marked by petty annoyances and frustrations. Expand your perspective and avoid getting lost in the minutiae of trivial disagreements. Keep your focus on the bigger picture (love, lifelong partnership) and maintain a healthy perspective on your relationship through humor, gratitude, and meaningful gestures.

Shared humor may not actually cure your marriage issues, but it probably won't hurt. Laughing is an instant stress reliever that also challenges perceptions. Recognizing the absurdity of a dilemma, the inherent dark humor of a catastrophe, or the irony of a situation can help couples cope with life's challenges. Laughing with your loved one is particularly rewarding because it connects you to a shared sensibility. Laughing creates intimacy and even reinforces a communal sense of our shared humanity. Consciously bring humor and lightness into your marriage with a date night out to a comedy club, or step up to the mike yourself. This is the single instance when it may be okay for one spouse to laugh at another.

It is a wonderful gift to have someone in your life who agrees to share it for the long haul. This is what makes marriage so special and different from all other relationships. Reminding yourself of this gift can help you to maintain a healthy perspective. It is essential to say "thank you," and not take your spouse, or their labors, for granted. Sometimes couples who have been together for a significant amount of time forget to say these simple words. However, everyone wants to be recognized for their contributions, even in cases where the effort is expected. So, even if your husband takes out the recycling every night because it is his designated responsibility, it might be a good idea to say "thanks."

In addition to verbalizing your appreciation, consider the positive impact of communicating gratitude through simple, yet meaningful gestures. If your wife loves tennis, pick up a couple of canisters of tennis balls the next time you are browsing at a sports store. If your husband dreads taking the dog out for his evening walk, volunteer for the chore. Create a special meal for your partner, which is both a concrete form of nourishment, as well as a symbolic act that communicates caring and love. Even if you don't consider yourself a cook, occasionally attempting to make your partner's favorite foods and carving out time to sit down with him or her and enjoy it can be an intimate experience. With imagination as your guide, embed love and gratitude into every day.

Attending to your spouse will encourage reciprocation and create a supportive environment that promotes change. Strong marriages do not happen accidentally; they reflect the hard work and emotional consciousness of both spouses. Designing your ideal marriage is not a solitary or linear process. It is a multifaceted journey that evolves as you and your spouse change throughout your life together. Listening with your heart, communicating anger responsibly, cultivating sacred time, and keeping love in the foreground of your relationship are infallible tactics for making sure your adventure stays on the right path.

MIKE ROBBINS has inspired tens of thousands of people to reach new levels of awareness and success, both personally and professionally through his talks, seminars, and writing. He teaches people to be more grateful, appreciative, and authentic with others and themselves. Robbins is the author of the bestselling book, *Focus on the Good Stuff: The Power of Appreciation*, and the new book, *Be Yourself, Everyone Else Is Already Taken*. He is also a contributing author to *Chicken Soup for the Single Parent's Soul* and *Thirty Things To Do When You Turn Thirty* from Sellers Publishing.

BE THEIR BIGGEST FAN AND GREATEST CRITIC

Mike Robbins

I saw Rev. Michael Bernard Beckwith, founder and spiritual director of the Agape International Spiritual Center in Los Angeles, perform a recommitment ceremony for a married couple at one of his services a few years back and it blew me away. He looked at the husband and said, "Your job is to be her biggest fan and her greatest critic for the purpose of her spiritual development." He then turned to the wife and said the same thing to her about him. As simple a concept as this was for me to understand, I had never heard anyone say it quite like this. What he said fully registered with me, and I was moved deeply and began to cry. I realized that so often I'd struggled with what felt like my conflicting desires to share my love and appreciation with Michelle, my wife, and also to let her know when something didn't work for me or when I thought she was "off" in a certain aspect of her life. I noticed that I was usually quite "hot or cold" about this — either being totally focused on appreciating her or completely focused on being critical of her (or withholding my feedback so as to not hurt her feelings, which in turn resulted in my withholding some of my love and appreciation from her).

Hearing Rev. Michael say this made me realize that both of these things — appreciation and feedback — are essential not only for the health of a marriage, but for the personal and spiritual growth of each person in the relationship as well.

These two important things — being our spouse's greatest fan and biggest critic — can be seen as opposites when we look at them from a superficial perspective. But, upon deeper reflection, it becomes clear that they're intricately connected and fundamentally important for the well-being and success of a marriage.

Our ability (or often inability) to express our genuine appreciation for our husband or wife is directly related to how safe or comfortable we feel giving them critical feedback. In other words, the more open we are to giving and receiving honest (and sometimes negative) feedback from our spouse, the more capacity we have to express and experience genuine love and appreciation with them. And, when we don't feel safe or comfortable giving them honest feedback (or we just aren't willing to), it actually diminishes our ability to acknowledge them in a real way, and it ultimately damages our marriage.

How To Be Their Biggest Fan

Being our spouse's biggest fan means that we focus on what we appreciate about them (i.e., look for the good stuff) and are willing to let them know how we feel in a loving and generous way. It's essential that we acknowledge them without agenda or because we want something in return (for example, doing something for them so they'll do something for us, say something to us, or even like or love us more). Acknowledgments with agendas are manipulations, not acts of true appreciation. Being their biggest fan is about celebrating them, recognizing their value (whether or not we like or agree with them all the time, which we won't), believing in them, and reminding them of their greatness.

Here are five key aspects of practicing the power of appreciation with your spouse to be their biggest fan:

1. Look for and Expect Good Stuff

Our expectations have a big impact on our marriage. In order to appreciate, inspire, and ultimately empower our spouse — we must have positive expectations of them. We almost always get what we expect.

Having high expectations of other people, especially our partner, can be a little tricky. We've all gotten "burned" or hurt in the past when we expected something specific from someone (particularly someone we were in a romantic relationship with) and that person didn't come through. Additionally, some of us know that our high expectations can put undue pressure and stress on those close to us and ultimately have a disempowering and negative effect on them. There's a fine line between having positive expectations that empower our spouse and putting perfection demands on them that they can't achieve and that will stress them out.

For us to impact our spouse in a positive way, we have to work out this balance of expectation and pressure for ourselves and adjust it accordingly, based upon our personality, our relationship, and the situation. Regardless of the adjustments that we must make, it's important for us to understand the impact of our positive expectations on our partner and our marriage.

If you expect your spouse to let you down, flake out on things, disappoint you, upset you, and more — guess what you'll often find? However, if you expect them to be great, to do the right thing, to treat you well, to keep their agreements with you, and to be a fantastic partner, and more, the chances are much better that they will.

2. Be Genuine and Speak from Your Heart

Phony appreciation doesn't work. We must be real when we thank, compliment, or acknowledge our partner. The more our appreciation comes from our heart, the more likely it will have a meaningful impact on our spouse.

Here are some simple tips to make sure your acknowledgments are genuine:

- Be specific.

- Look them in the eye.

- Be spontaneous and creative.

- Take a deep breath, slow down, and speak from a deep place within you.

- Say what you mean, and mean what you say.

Remember that most of us get somewhat nervous or awkward (either a lot or a little) when we acknowledge people, even our spouse, in a heartfelt and genuine way. One sign of a real acknowledgment is that one or both of the people exhibits signs of being emotionally impacted in some way (nervous, touched, moved to tears, etc.). It's totally normal and very appropriate to have some kind of emotional reaction when you're acknowledging your partner. It just means that you're human, that you care, that you love them, and that you're being vulnerable. These are all good things, even if such feelings are a little uncomfortable at times. Very often when Michelle and I acknowledge each other, especially publicly, one or both of us will blush, find ourselves getting a little nervous, or even have tears in our eyes.

3. Thank Them All the Time

Thanking our spouse is one of the most important things we can do — both in a reactive way (for things they've done) and in a proactive way (just because we love and appreciate them). As long as we do it in a genuine way and without any agenda, we can never show our partner too much appreciation. I've yet to talk to a husband who says to me, "Boy, my wife just thanks me way too much, it really gets on my nerves." And I've never heard a wife say, "That husband of mine, he just appreciates me all day long, it's really annoying." Sadly, the opposite is true quite often and is usually one of the main reasons for conflicts, fights, and ultimately divorce.

Whether we do it in a really big and dramatic way, or a small and simple way, one of the greatest gifts we can give to our significant other is to thank them and to do so often. When I'm on the road speaking and I get a voice mail message from Michelle thanking me for taking care of our family, it makes me feel great. On those same trips, when I take the time to let her know how much I appreciate her taking care of our girls, our home, and our family, she tells me how much that means to her and how much she appreciates it.

4. Let Them Know Their Positive Impact on You

One of the best ways for us to acknowledge our spouse is to let them know the positive impact they have on us. Instead of saying, "You're wonderful," you could say, "I feel so lucky to be married to you — being with you makes me feel loved, appreciated, and cared for." Or instead of saying, "You look good," say, "Wow, being around you right now excites me and turns me on."

When we let our partner know the positive impact they have on us, we're sharing our deepest truths with them and therefore our appreciation has more power. When we tell them that they're "great" or "smart" or cite other positive qualities, we're actually making judgments — *positive* judgments, yes, but judgments nonetheless.

We could just as easily say they're "bad" or "stupid." When we share the positive impact they have on us, we're not simply giving them our judgmental opinion in a positive way, we're telling them who they are in our eyes, what they've done or what quality they have that we appreciate, and, most importantly, how that positive action or quality has made our life better.

5. Acknowledge Them for No Apparent Reason
Acknowledging our spouse for "no reason" is the ultimate form of proactive appreciation and is something that is vital for the success of our marriages. Michelle really taught me the power of this.

When we first started dating, Michelle sat me down and gave me a long list of things she liked and didn't like. She was very straightforward about it, which I appreciated. It was sort of like a "road map" to making her happy (which is a great thing to share with your partner if you haven't done so already). One small thing that Michelle mentioned to me in that conversation stuck out. She said, "I really like flowers. But I especially like flowers for no reason."

A week or so later I saw a flower stand and remembered what she had said. I bought Michelle some flowers, "for no reason," and brought them to her apartment, even though I really wasn't sure what her reaction would be. I gave her the flowers and she loved it. I mean, she really loved it. She got so excited — her face lit up, she smiled, and she actually started jumping up and down. It was wonderful to see her so happy. Because she expressed her appreciation so visibly and so immediately, I found myself searching for flowers wherever I went so that I could bring them to her and make her happy.

I began buying her flowers, "for no reason," all the time. She appreciated the flowers and me so much, and as a result she got more of what she wanted. To this day, I get flowers for Michelle on a regular basis. She "trained" me with her positive reaction and it ended up being a true win-win.

When we take the time to look for, find, and acknowledge what we appreciate about our spouse, we give them one of the greatest gifts of all — our gratitude!

APPRECIATION EXERCISE
"Create" the day with your spouse

This is a very powerful practice that Michelle and I came up with a few years ago (and one that I share with friends and clients all the time). This practice is one that you can do with your spouse each morning (or as often as possible). You say to them, "Who you are for me today is . . ." and then you "create" them with such words of acknowledgment as "loving, powerful, beautiful, wonderful, fun, etc." This practice is all about the creative power of our words and the magical power of appreciation. You want your acknowledgment to be genuine, but it's also important to remember that whatever you focus on, think about, feel, and say has the ability to manifest and create. Michelle and I also add more pieces to the process;

*after saying, "Who you are for me today is . . .," we also say,
"Something I love about you is . . .," "Something I love about
your body is . . .," "Something I love about our relationship
is . . .," and even "Something I love about myself is . . ." For
the final piece of this practice, we say, "Today I choose you!"
Creating the day not only starts your day off in a very positive
and powerful way, it's an amazing way to connect with and
acknowledge your partner from your heart.*

How To Be Their Greatest Critic

Being our spouse's greatest critic means that we're willing to say
things that might be scary or may even potentially hurt their feelings,
but we do so anyway (with kindness) because we're interested in
having a relationship with depth, trust, and authenticity. Being
their greatest critic is not about being critical or judgmental
(both of which can be hurtful and harmful to us, them, and our
marriage), it's about being able to share things that get between us
(the things we withhold from them or are afraid to admit), and also
about giving them feedback that can help them be the best possible
version of themselves (i.e., supporting their personal and spiritual
development). It can be a slippery slope for many of us on either
side of this equation, but for our marriage to thrive, we must have
the freedom to give and receive honest feedback from our spouse
in a productive and open way.

Here are some simple steps and reminders you can use to make sure
that your feedback is effective, honest, and positive.

• Ask permission.

Make sure that you have their permission to give them feedback and that they're open to receiving it in that moment. Even if their permission may be "granted," it's important to respect and honor them and to make sure they're open to hearing what you have to say when you have to say it. For example, you can simply say, "I want to talk about something important. Do I have your permission to be totally honest with my feedback?" Then, wait for them to respond.

• Acknowledge any fear or hesitation on your part.

If you're nervous or hesitant about giving your spouse feedback, make sure to acknowledge your fear as a way to be real and vulnerable. Doing this will take the "edge" off of the situation and will allow you to relax a bit and connect more with them — human to human. I will often say to Michelle, "Wow, I notice I am feeling scared to say this, but I feel it's important," or something similar to that.

• Let them know your positive intention.

Make sure you're clear with them up front about why you're giving them the feedback and what kind of positive impact you hope to achieve. An example for this would be, "I want to talk to you about something that's been bothering me and may be a little touchy, but my intention in bringing this up is so we can be even closer and support each other in an even more loving way."

• Let them know what they're doing well.

Point out their strengths and specifically acknowledge qualities and interactions that you appreciate. Don't "blow smoke," but make sure to let them know what's going well so that they do not hear the feedback as an overall assessment that everything is "all bad." For example, if you're giving them feedback about something that they're doing around the house that you don't like or about something you'd like them to do more or less of in general (listen, talk, drink, give you a back rub, etc.), make sure to point out, in a genuine way, some of the things you *appreciate* about what they do around the house or in general, in addition to giving them your critical feedback.

• Use "I" statements.

When giving feedback, make sure to let your spouse know that this is only your opinion, not the "truth," and avoid accusing them of anything or even using the word "you" if at all possible. For example, instead of telling them you think they should watch less TV or not spend so much time on their computer or phone, you can say, "I notice when you're on your cell phone at night, I feel sad and disconnected from you."

• Let them know what you want.

Make sure to be very clear about the changes, actions, or specific outcome you would like to see. The more clear and positive you are about what you want to see, the more likely it is that they'll understand what you're saying and hear what you want. If your feedback simply focuses on what they did wrong and you don't give them any suggestions or make any requests about how to change or improve, they're not left with anything positive they can take away from your feedback. Make sure to stay focused on solutions in a positive way. As an example, if you find yourself feeling like you and your spouse aren't spending as much quality time together as you'd like, you may request that you schedule specific date nights each week and put them in your calendars at the beginning of each month.

• **Acknowledge them.**

Thank them for having the conversation with you, for listening, for being open, and for hearing you and your feedback. Often it takes a lot of courage for them to hang in and listen to what you have to say — especially if it's critical of them. Thanking them is a great way to fill them up and make sure your feedback "lands" in a positive and productive way. However the conversation goes, see if you can look them in the eye and say "thank you" from your heart, for their willingness to engage with you in an honest, open, and sometimes difficult conversation. The more kindness and love you bring to these situations and conversations, the easier they will be throughout your marriage.

These simple steps are the ones that Michelle and I use (or try to remember to use) when we have a conflict, want to give each other some feedback, or have a difficult conversation with one another. The more volatile the situation, the more challenging it can be to use these steps, but also the more important it is to remember them. The two most essential keys to giving effective feedback to our partner are honesty and kindness. When we put honesty and kindness up front, the chances of our interactions and conversations being productive and positive are high. We have to remember to not manage their emotions or sugarcoat things simply because we're afraid they might get upset. It's part of our job as their spouse to give them loving, caring, genuine feedback. If we don't, who else will?

FEEDBACK EXERCISE
Release Your "Withholds"

A "withhold" is something you've been holding onto with your spouse that you haven't shared with them — hurts, resentments, fears, an apology, an acknowledgment, or anything else. Creating the time and space to communicate these "withholds" is an incredibly powerful and liberating thing to do, even though it can be a little scary. (Michelle and I do this on a regular basis.) One of you goes first and says to the other, "There's something I've withheld from you." The other person responds by saying, "Okay, would you like to tell me?" Then you express your "withhold" with as much honesty, vulnerability, and responsibility as possible (i.e., using "I" statements, owning your feelings, etc.).

For example, Michelle might say to me, "I noticed the other day when we were all together as a family, it felt to me like you didn't really want to be there; that made me feel sad." My job is to listen to her with as much openness as possible, not to react, and to just say "thank you" when she's done, even if I don't agree or have a specific response. For this technique to work and be safe for both people, we have to be able to share our withholds with each other without any specific response or feedback in the moment. It's best to do this back and forth until both of you have shared all of your withholds. When you're totally done, one or both of you may want to talk about some of the things that were said, but that isn't always necessary (many of them cease to be an issue once they're acknowledged). This is not about debate or someone being right or wrong, this is about being able to share how you're feeling and what you've been withholding as a way to release it and in order to give your spouse some necessary feedback.

Being our spouse's biggest fan and greatest critic may seem a bit counterintuitive or contradictory on the surface. However, as we've discussed here, it is our ability to both appreciate and give feedback to our partner in an authentic way that allows us to have the kind of marriage we truly want — one filled with love, honesty, openness, and growth.

Have fun and remember to be kind, loving, and forgiving to yourself and your spouse along the way!

BARBARA DE ANGELIS, PH.D., is the author of fourteen #1 *New York Times* bestsellers (translated into twenty languages, 8 million copies sold worldwide), including *How to Make Love All the Time*, *What Women Want Men to Know*, *Secrets About Men Every Woman Should Know*, and *Are You the One for Me?* She is a pioneer in the field of personal transformation and she was one of the first nationally recognized female motivational speakers on television. She has been a frequent guest on *The Oprah Winfrey Show*, *The Today Show*, *Good Morning America*, and *The View*. She's contributed to *Chicken Soup for the Couple's Soul* and written regularly for *Cosmopolitan*, *Ladies' Home Journal*, *McCall's*, *Redbook*, and *Family Circle*.

MAKING THE CHOICE
TO LOVE NOW

Barbara De Angelis, Ph.D.

Of all the wonders life on earth has to offer, none is greater to me than Love. Love infuses life with meaning. It performs magic and miracles. It brings light where there was darkness and hope where there was despair. It is your greatest teacher, and your most constant blessing.

Love is a force more formidable than any other. It is invisible. It cannot be seen, nor measured, yet it is powerful enough to transform you in a moment and to offer you more joy than any material possession could. Once love is yours, no one can take it away from you. Only you can relinquish it, if you wish.

Love is the magician of the Universe. It creates everything out of nothing. One moment, it isn't there, and the next — POOF — it appears in all its splendor, and you greet it with amazement. And what delights it produces out of thin air — smiles, laughter, goose-bumps, hot flashes, tender words, silly names, happy tears, and most of all, life. Love produced you. Without it, you wouldn't be here at all.

Love's greatest gift is its ability
to make everything it touches sacred.

Love sanctifies life. *Where love is, you are given a glimpse of the sacred.* You rise above your humanness and see the world through heavenly eyes. Your child, your beloved, your dog or cat, your garden, or whatever it is that you love appears adorable, precious, supremely beautiful, and somehow perfect in spite of its imperfections. And love also consecrates time and place and possession, bestowing special stature upon them: the day you first met your husband; the anniversary of your wedding; the special bench in the park where you go to talk; the rocking chair in which you nursed your child; the old afghan your grandmother made you; your little girl's first note that said "I love you, Mommy"; these become sacred artifacts commemorating the presence of love in your life.

But most of all, I believe that love offers you an opportunity for deep, spiritual awakening, for when you love, the usual boundaries, which separate you from something else, dissolve; you transcend the illusion of separation that defines human existence, and you experience Oneness. Suddenly, you are no longer alone in the Universe. There is a flow between your being and the being of whomever you are loving. All that is you is pouring out into them, and all that they are is pouring out into you. Your souls are dancing together.

This is the power of love — *it takes you on a journey from separation to Oneness.* It penetrates the normal boundaries in which you live, the boundaries that make you feel like "you," distinct and unrelated to anyone or anything else. You know that you are not your husband or wife or dog or friend or the sky. And yet, in those very real moments of love, "you" turns into "us," something infinitely more fulfilling than you alone.

In this way, love creates an unlimited experience with no boundaries, no edges. It allows you to travel out of yourself.

ALL LOVE IS AN OUT-OF-BODY EXPERIENCE.

You may not have ever considered yourself a spiritual person, but every true experience of love is spiritual, as your spirit touches the spirit of someone or something else. **Love becomes your doorway into the divine.**

Love is the ultimate method for creating real moments, because love forces you to practice mindfulness. It pulls you into an eternal present. It focuses all of your attention on what you are experiencing, and it requires that you surrender to it. The better you become at loving, the more real moments you'll be able to create.

An intimate relationship is a sacred opportunity for you to use love as a path for personal and spiritual transformation. It forces you to open where you were closed, to feel where you were numb, to express what was silent, to reach out where you would retreat. *It's easy to feel like you are a loving and enlightened person when you are alone, but when you get into a relationship, you come face to face with every emotional limitation you possess.*

Relationships are an instant and continual training ground. They insist that you look in the mirror at yourself, they reveal all the parts of you that are not loving. They show you your dark side. They knock on the door of your heart, demanding that you open the places you've kept locked. And then, every day and night, they give you an opportunity to practice love, to stretch yourself beyond what is comfortable, and to keep doing it better.

Using Your Relationship as a Path

I chose to follow the path of love at a very early age, for I knew it would lead me to the real moments of meaning I was searching for. It has been an exciting, mysterious, often painful but always liberating journey. For a long time, I wasn't very good at loving. I made many mistakes. I hurt myself and I hurt others. But slowly, I learned how to use love and relationship as a sacred path of learning and transformation. And I was finally blessed to find a man who was willing to travel that same path with me, and share the adventure.

All great creations begin with a vision. Before an artist paints, he has a vision of the picture in his mind. Before an architect designs a building, she has a vision of what it should look like. Before a musician writes a piece of music, he hears the finished piece in his head. Vision fuels the birth of all that is produced with love.

IF YOU DON'T HAVE A VISION OF WHERE YOU WANT YOUR
RELATIONSHIP TO GO, IT WON'T GO ANYWHERE.

Being in a relationship without both agreeing on its destination is like trying to take a long road trip without a map — you're going to get lost over and over again, and you're not going to enjoy the ride. To use your relationship as a path, both you and your partner must create a shared vision of the purpose of your being together, and then make a sincere commitment to living that vision. *Vision helps us get through difficult times.* It focuses our awareness on the destination and encourages us to keep going, even when we feel lost or disheartened. It is the vision of the career you want to have that helps you study, write papers, and work hard through college. It is the vision of yourself as a mother holding your newborn baby in your arms that gives you courage to get through the pain of labor. **It is the vision of your relationship as a transformational path that will give you and your partner the strength, patience, and perseverance to travel the High Road of Love together.**

Here are several truths that make up the vision my husband and I share of our relationship:

1. **We have been brought together for the purpose of helping each other grow, and we will be each other's teacher.**
2. **Our relationship is a precious gift — it will take us through whatever we need to learn to become more conscious, loving human beings.**
3. **The challenges and difficulties we experience will always illuminate our most needed lessons.**

Because we have made a commitment to accept this purposeful

vision of our love, we experience the struggles and problems we encounter in a sacred context. When we are angry at one another and argue, when we get frustrated and feel like turning away, our vision shines like a beacon of light in the fog, reminding us that there is a higher purpose to the everyday difficulties we're challenged by. *We remember that we have chosen to travel together for a reason, and by remembering, we can more quickly release the anger, move beyond the hurt, forgive, and find our eternal bond of love that is always present underneath.*

It is easy to forget the true purpose of your relationship when you are busy with work, children, and family obligations. And when you forget your purpose as a couple, you lose your way. A relationship that has lost its way will stop moving and growing, for it won't know where it is supposed to go.

Feeding the Soul of Your Relationship

You need real moments of intimacy, of oneness, to nourish the spirit of your love so that it will continue to grow. Sharing these moments with your partner reminds you both of your timeless connection, your purpose in finding one another, and thus gives you renewed vision and courage to get you through the challenges of living together.

REAL MOMENTS ARE THE LIFEBLOOD OF
INTIMATE RELATIONSHIPS.

Without real moments, the soul of your relationship will die. You may still choose to ignore your lack of fulfillment and stay together, but your relationship will exist as an empty shell, an arrangement of convenience you make in order to not be alone.

Having real moments of intimacy doesn't mean just being with someone. It's what *happens* when you are together that makes it a real moment of love. You can be physically together and be emotionally a million miles away because you are not in the moment. Or you can create a real moment on the phone, even though you're calling from a thousand miles away, simply because you are letting the boundaries go and sharing the deepest parts of your heart.

Most relationships I see around me are suffering from real-moment deprivation. It's not that the two people don't love each other — they do. But *they don't feel the love as deeply as they should,* because they aren't giving the love opportunities to surface and to be experienced without distraction. *They aren't having enough real moments together.*

Most people look at a relationship like a possession — "I have a car; I have a job; I have a relationship." The relationship becomes something to *get,* and once that goal has been obtained, they don't put much time or energy into it.

**MARRIAGE IS NOT A NOUN, IT'S A VERB.
IT ISN'T SOMETHING YOU GET, IT'S SOMETHING YOU DO.**

Marriage is not a wedding ring, or a piece of paper that proves you are husband and wife, or a party that says you've been married for twenty-five years. Marriage is a *behavior* — it is how you love and honor your partner every day. You aren't married because the county or your family thinks you are. *The real act of marriage takes place in the heart,* not in a ballroom or church or synagogue. It is a choice you make, not just on your wedding day, but over and over again, and that choice is reflected in the way you treat your husband or wife.

Your marriage is renewed and reconsecrated every time you share a real moment together.

We avoid real moments in relationships because if we aren't used to them, they can be frightening in their intensity.

Have you ever sat with someone you loved late at night, sharing your thoughts, your hopes, your secret feelings? At first, you're just talking, but at some point, enough doors have been opened, enough connections have been made, and something greater than your two individual selves is created. It is tangible. You both can feel it. It is a space you occupy together, a sacred space that emerges when enough truth has been spoken and acknowledged. Suddenly, you feel your connectedness as strong as anything you've ever felt. You are experiencing a real moment.

All at once you realize that you are out of control. Your boundaries have melted, and the usual protections you have are dissolving, leaving you uncomfortable in your vulnerability. You are being seen without your masks, your innermost emotions are being witnessed by someone else. The sanctity of your personal space has been penetrated.

Ironically, this is actually the definition of love, when you allow your soul to touch someone else's. **If you are not good at trusting and letting go, you will pull away from the moment, and turn away from the love, for fear that you will lose yourself in it. You will crave retreat from your partner, maybe even from the relationship. Or perhaps you will just avoid intimacy and relationship entirely, knowing that without it, those terrifying moments of vulnerability cannot happen.**

What are you running from? Your own nakedness. What are you afraid of? Losing your edges, your ego, and being swallowed up by a force more powerful than you. It is a kind of death — the death of your separateness, the death of your illusions about yourself.

Many of us spend our lives playing hide and seek with ourselves — we do whatever we can to avoid facing our truth and exploring our shadows. *If this has been your agenda, you will be terrified of true, deep love and the real moments of surrender it requires of you.* And you will find ways to flee from them.

Loving may appear to be an emotional risk, but in reality, it isn't a risk at all.

YOU NEVER LOSE BY LOVING.
YOU ALWAYS LOSE BY HOLDING BACK LOVE.

. . . The real risk is in living with someone year after year without truly knowing their soul, or them knowing yours.

. . . The real risk is having a marriage based on materialism and superficiality, and avoiding those kinds of human connection that are truly significant.

. . . The real risk is being in a relationship without real moments.

Finding Your Ability To Feel Again

Experiencing intimacy with your beloved requires that you open yourself totally to the moment, not just by showing up physically, but by *showing up emotionally.* You aren't pretending to listen, while thinking of something else; you aren't reading the paper while she is trying to reach out; you aren't going through the motions of loving, but feeling numb — you are fully present with him or with her. After all, if *you* aren't *there* in the moment, then who is there to love, to connect with, to be intimate with?

Being there emotionally in the moment means knowing how to fully *feel* your feelings.

> **THE ABILITY TO FEEL LOVE IS BASED ON THE**
> **ABILITY TO FEEL . . . PERIOD.**

You can't feel love or happiness or contentment if you have forgotten how to feel. Many of us were robbed of our ability to feel as children. Now, as adults, not feeling has become an old habit — we suppress, edit, and deny our emotions on a regular basis. We respond to requests for connection with phrases like: *"Not now," "I don't want to talk about it," "Nothing's wrong," "Aren't you ever satisfied?"* We drink alcohol, take drugs, eat junk food, work incessantly, and watch too much TV, all in an attempt to numb ourselves. Thus we carry years of frozen feelings inside of our hearts, and when it comes time to connect, to be intimate, even if we want to, we don't know how.

FINDING YOUR ABILITY TO FEEL AGAIN IS THE FIRST STEP TOWARDS EXPERIENCING TRUE INTIMACY WITH YOUR PARTNER AND CREATING REAL MOMENTS IN RELATIONSHIP.

To do this, you need to defrost the ice around your heart. Cry all the tears you never shed; release the old rage from your body; find your voice and give it permission to say all the things it has kept silent for so long. *The more you work on healing your emotional wounds, the easier it will be for you to love.*

I've spent my whole life developing powerful and effective techniques to break down emotional walls. I needed them first to heal myself, and then to share with my students. There are many other teachers and therapists who also offer their own methods for emotional healing. **Use us. We are here to help you find your way back to your self.**

"You learn to speak by speaking, to study by studying, to run by running, to work by working; and just so, you learn to love . . . by loving. All those who think to learn in any other way deceive themselves." — Saint Francis de Sales

How do you begin to experience more real moments in loving? **You begin.** No putting it off until your next vacation, or Saturday night, or until you finish this chapter. *Now* is the time. No waiting until it feels right, or until you think you'll be better at it. *It will never feel right until you do it, and you won't get better at it until you start.*

Loving well is a skill, just like playing an instrument, or operating a computer, or cooking — the more you do it, the better you get. Creating real moments of intimacy takes practice. You could listen to every tape I've recorded, or attend every seminar on relationships that is available, but you still wouldn't be good at loving. **Loving is the only way to get good at loving.**

It *is* difficult to love well, but the more we work on it, loving becomes a habit. You no longer have to remind yourself to tell your partner how much you appreciate him — you just find yourself doing it; he doesn't have to be asked to share his feelings — he volunteers them on his own. Suddenly, it feels more natural for you both to love, to give, to open than it does to not love and to hold back. And the more you each give, the easier it gets, until there's no more effort. Finally, what's become easy begins to deepen as you and your beloved step out of the way and allow love to simply flow through each of you to the other.

Here is one of the most important truths to remember:

LOVE IS A CHOICE YOU MAKE FROM MOMENT TO MOMENT.

You *choose* to love, to express it, to share it, to show it. You do not wait to be seized by an overwhelming feeling of love that propels you into action. You don't wait to say, "I love you," until the words are bursting out of your mouth. You don't wait to give your wife a hug until you can't physically control yourself. *You make these gestures because you remember that you love this person, and because you know that by choosing to love, you will not only make your partner happy, but you will focus your own attention on the love you feel and bring yourself joy.*

Making the Choice To Love Now

It is an unfortunate part of our human nature that we take what we have for granted until we lose it, and then weep for what can no longer be ours, and berate ourselves for the time we wasted.

IF YOU HAVE SOMEONE SPECIAL IN YOUR LIFE, DON'T WAIT TO START LOVING HIM OR HER.

Do not put it off for even one day. You do not, as your mind would like you to believe, have all the time in the world. Whoever loves you is only on loan from God, and he or she could be taken from you at any moment.

Do the people in your life really know how much you love them, and how deeply you need them? Don't wait to celebrate them until they pass from the earth. Don't save up your words for their funeral. Don't put off loving them with abandon. **Make the choice to love now.**

DEBRA GALANT is both a new media entrepreneur and a novelist. She has written hundreds of articles and columns for the *New York Times* on topics ranging from kitchen envy to nudist colonies. She is the highly regarded author of *Rattled*, a Book Sense pick and a *New York Times* Editors' Choice selection, and *Fear and Yoga in New Jersey*, also a Book Sense pick. Her most recent novel, *Cars from a Marriage*, is published by St. Martin's. Galant is also the founder and editor of *Baristanet.com*, named the Best Placeblog in America in 2007. She has written for *New York* magazine, *Barron's*, and *Worth*, and she contributed commentary to NPR's "All Things Considered."

THE NUPTIAL CAR

Debra Galant

"Just Married," proclaims the back window in shaving cream. Cans trail behind, clanking merrily. Passersby honk and smile. The groom is wearing black, the bride white, like wedding cake toppers but finally sitting down, glad to be off their feet, finally, having waved goodbye and started off on their fabulous adventure as Man and Wife.

The journey of a thousand fights begins.

Freeze this moment — the nuptial car — place it carefully in a mental scrapbook, and remember it for later.

Remember it when he's driving too fast down the highway and your nails are digging into the armrest. You've glanced over at the speedometer three times and seen the needle hovering 15 miles above the posted limit. The first time, you just look. The second time, you look and sigh significantly. The third time, you mention it, and he presses down harder on the gas pedal.

Remember it when you mention it again, and he swerves across two lanes to the shoulder, turns the car off, folds his arms, and says tersely, "Okay, you drive." Which, of course, is impossible — you being terrified to drive on highways and all.

Remember it when the water pump goes or the carburetor or the little electrical panel that controls the ignition, and the money that it will take to fix it is the money you'd planned to spend on a new rug for the living room or a bed-and-breakfast weekend. When you are debating whether this is the end of this particular car, whether you are throwing good money after bad, whether you really need to replace it, and whether this time, maybe, you should replace it with a car with automatic transmission, rather than a stick, which only he can drive.

Remember it when he sighs, the stick shift question quite obviously raising phallic issues, which will come back to haunt you later, even if you do win, and the new car has automatic transmission.

Try to remember this picture, the happy young newlyweds — just try! — when the two of you are driving somewhere far from home and it begins to snow. Softly at first, in delicate laceworks, and then in increasingly bigger clumps, which the windshield wipers swipe at vainly, until finally snow has blanketed the whole world and visibility has narrowed to a saucer-sized sliver of sloppy glass. Remember this when you are huddled into a tight ball of frayed nerves, and even he is leaning forward in an unfamiliar posture of fierce concentration, and you are arguing that you must get off the road, immediately, find a hotel, any hotel, and he insists that he's got the whole thing under control, there's only about sixty miles to go, and suddenly the car goes into a fishtail.

But no, who can think of that wedding day, the white dress, his smile at the altar, the first dance, when the car has become a projectile and the world is a sudden blur of headlights and your pounding heart? No, you are lucky if you can hold onto that picture afterwards, when the car has righted itself, and you are safe, but he still insists that everything is under control, there's no reason to stop.

He screams, "Do you think I want to die? Do you think you're the only one who wants to live?" But it is beginning to dawn on you that although you both want this thing — life — you would like a wider margin. Apparently he is comfortable with about an inch between life and oblivion, and you would prefer at least a foot. And it's that space, that eleven inches, which will dog your marriage forever, until the hearse at last takes one of you away.

Because you really do want the same thing, you know? You are heading in the same direction, at least at first.

It is true that men are loath to stop for directions, but does he pull over, uncomplainingly, when you say you need to go to the bathroom, and it's just been an hour since your last stop? If so, put a tally mark in the plus column. These are little things, but they need to be counted.

Does he go out when you're pregnant and have a craving for Chinese dumplings at 11:00 p.m. in the dead of winter? Does he volunteer to drive to Chuck E. Cheese when you are at that stage of life when your offspring are invited weekly to deafening orgies of pizza and arcade games? Does he take the car to the inspection station? Remember when your car is due for an oil change?

If so, add four more tally marks.

This may help when the third summons comes with the court date for the four-point speeding violation, followed by the letter from the insurance company with the new renewal rate.

Try to refrain from finger wagging if you accompany him to court and stand in line with him to wait for the prosecutor, who will bargain the offense down to two points, with a fine and court costs of $500, payable as soon as the judge calls him up and accepts his guilty plea. Consider your husband's hangdog expression before the judge, his bent head, an acknowledgment that you are right, have always been right, and will always be right. Even though this contrition is not directed at you, specifically, you can imagine that it is.

Anyway, it might be all you're going to get.

And besides, he got one of those tickets after you screamed at him that he needed to come home immediately because Child #1 just provoked you to the point of murder.

Here is an activity the two of you can engage in quite happily. Try this any Saturday. Turn on the radio and listen as Click and Clack, the Tappet Brothers, impart marital advice to other married couples, whose automotive disagreements are different from yours, having to do with things like convertible tops and gearshift techniques. Laugh hard with Tom and Ray, and daydream about the hilarity that would ensue if you were to call the show with your own issues of automotive discord.

Here is another fun activity. Someday, when you're on a vacation or the kids are farmed out, go rent a convertible. Preferably a red one. Wear a scarf. Channel your inner Gina Lollobrigida. Under no circumstances think about Grace Kelly.

Here's one to do with the kids. Find a drive-in movie theater, bring along lawn chairs, park the car, turn on the speaker, and enjoy everything American car culture has to offer at the comfortable velocity of zero miles per hour.

And there are always the bumper cars on the boardwalk, where collisions are actually part of the fun.

But what happens when the collisions actually hurt? When your roads diverge? When the marriage feels like that car with the broken carburetor?

It could be the slow accretion of mileage: the realization that the only conversation you ever have anymore is about the division of to-do lists. Or an unexpected vehicle suddenly veering into your lane: the call from the other woman, like a stab in the heart, late at night.

This is when the picture of the nuptial vehicle, stored safely in your memory bank, becomes not a solace but a mockery.

There are no easy answers to the question of whether the car is too far gone to save.

I advise you to think about the miles you've traveled, your common history, what you've acquired together since driving off into that first sunset. It may be that the car has accumulated more than wear and tear. The trunk may be filled with all kinds of souvenirs. It might be time to open it up, take them out, turn them tenderly in your hands.

There may be too much history to simply junk the vehicle. Remember the lovingly cared-for roadsters in small-town Memorial Day parades. Just because it's old and dented and poorly maintained, doesn't mean a worn-out car, or marriage, can't be restored.

If you're lost in your marriage, pull over, and take out the maps. Spend some time studying them.

Talk.

Talk late into the night, as if the only thing you have is darkness and time, as if all that mattered was this journey. Talk as if nothing existed but your headlights and the metronome of your windshield wipers ticking off the seconds. Talk as if your life depended on it.

But if there's been a wreck, you'll probably require a qualified mechanic. By this, of course, I mean a marriage counselor. This can be expensive. But probably not as expensive as getting rid of the old car.

This will not be a quick fix. You will be asked to get under the car, with your partner, and look at the greasy underside of things. You will have to learn to change your own oil. You will have to report strange noises, even if they are intermittent. Don't be surprised if you wind up overhauling your whole engine, and studying the manuals for your parents' cars as well.

This could take years.

Remember, however, that two vehicles cannot occupy the same space at the same time. This is simple physics. Sometimes, somebody will have to make a choice.

If you are lucky, if your heart is strong and your partner is willing, if you have a good mechanic and enough money, you might wind up rebuilding that nuptial car. You will know where the dents were — even if they've been pounded out and airbrushed over. There might still be scary things in the rearview mirror.

But it could turn out even better than the one you started out in.

ABOUT THE EDITOR

MARK CHIMSKY-LUSTIG is editor-in-chief of the book division of Sellers Publishing. For eight years, he ran his own editorial consulting business. Previously he was executive editor and editorial director of Harper San Francisco and headed the paperback divisions at Little, Brown and Macmillan. In addition, he was on the faculty of New York University's Center for Publishing and for three years he served as the director of the book section of NYU's Summer Publishing Institute. He has edited a number of bestselling books and worked with such authors as Johnny Cash, Melody Beattie, Susie Bright, Robert Funk, Arthur Hertzberg, Beryl Bender Birch, and Robert Coles. He is an award-winning poet whose poetry and essays have appeared in *JAMA* (*The Journal of the American Medical Association*), *Three Rivers Poetry Journal,* and *Mississippi Review.* In 2009, he developed and compiled *Creating a Life You'll Love,* a *Maine Sunday Telegram* bestseller published by Sellers Publishing.

ACKNOWLEDGMENTS

Just like raising a child, putting together a new book "takes a village." For *Creating a Marriage You'll Love*, I want to express my gratitude to all the contributors who so generously agreed to write and donate original essays for this book or to allow us to reprint excerpts from their previously published books.

I want to thank Victoria Moran, Laurie Fox, Linda Chester, Patti Breitman, Jo-Lynne Worley, and Liza Dawson for helping to lead me to some of the wonderful contributors in this book.

My appreciation to Stephanie Coontz's *Marriage, a History* (Viking, 2005), which I consulted for the Introduction.

As with the first book in this series, *Creating a Life You'll Love*, this new book was a team effort. I want to thank all those on the Sellers team who believed in this project and helped to make it happen: Ronnie Sellers, Robin Haywood, Megan Hiller, Mary Baldwin, Charlotte Smith (production pro *extraordinaire*!), Jeff Hall, Diana Kipp, Cynthia Kurtz, Scott Lovejoy, Colin McGee, Karen Suprenant, Andy Sturtevant, Jo Ann Van Reenen, Melvin Weiner, Matt Davis, and Lisa Reitan. My thanks as well go to Rita Sowins for a beautiful cover and Cary Hull for her incisive proofreading.

For their heartfelt support through the years, I am indebted to my extended family: Joanna Laufer and Ken Schreiber, Haya Leah Molnar and Tom Okada, Dede Byster, Richard Morse, Susan RoAne, Marcia Marcus, Paul Gilman and Maxine Borowitz, Chuck Brown, Amanda Mecke and Mary Ann Zeman, Kimberly Gladman and Philip M. Jackson, Christine Dietz and Linda McKenney, Jane Sloven and Dr. Joe Py, Rick and Tirrell Kimball, Cindy Thompson and Matt Rawdon, and Clare and Dr. Irving Dunsky.

A special thank you to my parents, who instilled in me a love for the music of language and the magic of reading.

And I am grateful to my son and Revi for teaching me more than I thought I needed to know about the power of love.

CREDITS

ALSO AVAILABLE FROM SELLERS PUBLISHING:

Creating a Life You'll Love
An inspiring, thought-provoking collection of some
of the best commencement addresses of recent years
by such notables as Genevieve Bell, Wendell Berry,
Ken Burns, Thomas L. Friedman, Tess Gerritsen, Dana
Gioia, Tom Hanks, Molly Ivins, Barbara Kingsolver, Ray
Kurzweil, David Levering Lewis, David McCullough,
Harold Prince, Anna Quindlen, Anna Deavere Smith,
Karen Tse, and Muhammad Yunus. A perfect gift for
new graduates or anyone making a major life transition.

All royalties generated from the sale of this book will
be donated to nonprofit organizations dedicated to
HIV/AIDS prevention and research.

COMING IN FALL 2010:

Creating a Meal You'll Love
The newest collection in the "Creating" series, featuring
lively essays by a wide range of acclaimed food writers
describing gloriously unique meals.

All royalties generated from the sale of this book will be
donated to the nonprofit organization Share Our Strength®,
dedicated to ending childhood hunger in America.